WWW

## NCQ TITLES

| | |
|---|---|
| Legal Fictions | Time Pieces |
| Politics & Letters | Critical Paranoia |
| On Yeats: Upon a House | On Joyce: 3 easy essays |
| Drama & Democracy | On Eliot |
| Locating Theology | Literary Conversions |

### *Film-texts*

| | |
|---|---|
| A Trip to Rome | A Week in Venice |
| A Short Break in Budapest | Four Days in Athens |
| Magic in Prague | The Last Priest of Horus |
| WWW: the weekend that warped the world | |

### *Play-texts*

Darwin: an evolutionary entertainment
Strange Meetings & Shorts

### Eliotics

### *In preparation*

Rubbishing Hockney & other reviews
On Collecting Walter Benjamin
Autobiography & Class Consciousness
Considering Canterbury Cathedral

*Though each can be read independently,
these NCQ publications, taken together,
comprise a single hyper-text collection.*

# WWW

## THE WEEKEND THAT WARPED THE WORLD

a film-text

Bernard Sharratt

New Crisis Quarterly
2015

NEW CRISIS QUARTERLY

ncq@newcrisisquarterly.myzen.co.uk

First published 2015

In memory of
the indomitable
Dave Reason
1946-2014

This film-text was not written with actual film production in mind. In fact, it was originally conceived as an imagined three-part television transmission over a weekend, the broadcasts more or less matching the time-schema of the plot. It has seemed preferable, however, to present it now as simply a continuous film-script, somewhat longer perhaps than an average movie. And though it plays with a variety of media genres, it is still primarily intended to be read—and imagined. In particular, readers are invited to imagine the technology envisaged in the script, and its possible implementation and effects.

It was written in 1999, purely for the fun of it and to play around with both television and film forms that I enjoy and with computer developments I was then involved in.. Despite some recent developments, the 'advanced' computer technology and the related themes explored in the script remain, perhaps ominously, somewhat ahead of its time.

This film-text could also be read as a 'Cambridge & London' film within what later became a series of NCQ 'city' film-texts, variously set in Athens, Budapest, Prague, Rome, and Venice, with others perhaps still to come.

A film-text is a particularly suitable form for the 'New Crisis Quarterly' imprint, since that name revives the title of an extremely short-lived periodical, whose first, only, and final issue originally appeared in 1984, under the guise of my *The Literary Labyrinth*. Its editorial programme was to publish reviews of imagined books I didn't feel that I had the time actually to write, so its readers were cheerfully invited, if so inclined, to write those works themselves. In the same spirit, reading a film-text means that most of the work of imagining the film can be done by you, which is part of the fun of writing them. In this case, indeed, you might also want to experiment with some image-processing software along the way.

B.S.
May Day
2015

## 1. EXT. A STREET. MORNING.

WRITTEN: *[X-Files style: unobtrusive lower left corner:]*

FRIDAY : 10TH OCTOBER
10.01 A.M.

*An old brick wall in medium close-up. No music.*
*Very heavy rain. Rumbles of thunder.*

*Camera slowly tilts up the closed grey metal shutters of a cheap Indian*
*restaurant, taking in faded name on a board: Momtaz Curry House.*
*The word 'Momtaz' is also in lights above the window, off at present.*

*Shot proceeds further up the depressing brick wall*
*to an upstairs window frame badly in need of maintenance.*
*Rain lashing against the wall and window.*

*We could be in any depressing Northern English town*
*— or film. Almost grey monochrome. Still no music. Rain only.*

## 2. INTERIOR. A ROOM.

*Shot moves through the dirty window pane  [Citizen Kane]*
*to show an extremely dingy bed-sit room in which*
*CHRISSIE is discovered: attractive 17 year old girl, brunette,*
*wrapped in a thread-bare woolly jumper over a crumpled nightdress,*
*huddled on an unmade bed.*

*Pan shows : large rickety wooden wardrobe. Cracked wall mirror.*
*Two shabby luggage cases on the floor. Orange box as bedside table.*
*Not much else.*
*Could be a drug den, white slave brothel, every parent's nightmare.*
*Is actually a student's digs.*

*Use single 'hand-held' 'amateur' camera for the following:*

*Chrissie is talking into a phone.*
*With a pronounced but artificial Liverpudlian accent.*

CHRISSIE

Yea, I know—Yea, I'll be fine—
Stop worryin', will ya—No need to send out the
rossers. OK, gorra go now. All de best fer
yer birthday. 'Tra Debbie, see ya Sunday.

*Chrissie puts down the phone. It is a very smart mobile phone.*

*Chrissie looks at battered bedside alarm-clock on the orange box:
digital, in form of an orange. Shakes it. Rapid and awkward camera
zoom shows it has stopped at 09.27 a.m. Shaking makes the digital
counter spin very fast forward and the alarm goes off stridently—.*

CHRISSIE

Sod it!

*She moves to behind the open wardrobe door and starts rapidly to get
undressed. The Camera tries to follow her, but its, and our, view is
obstructed by the open wardrobe door. [Peeping Tom]
The Camera manoeuvres to try to get a better view.
The wardrobe door swings to block it, thumping the camera.*

*Camera swings round, trying to get a viewing angle through the mirror.
Before it succeeds, Chrissie reappears from behind the wardrobe door,
fully dressed, in very fashionable street gear. She is now a blonde.*

*She goes to a shabby suitcase and takes out a stunningly state-of-the-
art-and-beyond tablet computer and furls it into its pink umbrella
mode: that is, a slim handle, with a pink umbrella top, slides out of one
edge of the tablet, which then rolls itself up out of sight into the handle.*

*She leaves the room, cheerfully swinging the computer-umbrella,
and singing in a very broad artificial Yorkshire accent:*

On Ilkley Moor Ba' Ta-at
W'ere hast tha bin sin I saw thee?
W'ere hast tha bin sin I saw thee?
On Ilkley Moor Ba' Tat
On Ilkley Moor Ba' Tat—

## 3. EXT. STREET.
*[standard camera action from now on]*

*Chrissie comes out of a door next to the Momtaz
into a narrow side street. Grey rain is still lashing down.
A few young people are hurrying miserably through the rain.*

*Chrissie dances on the sidewalk and gutters with the (computer-)
pink umbrella. She hums the 'Singing in the Rain' tune.*

*Shot follows her to end of street, where, very abruptly:*

## 4. EXT. KING'S PARADE, CAMBRIDGE, UK.

*Glorious view of King's College Chapel, Cambridge,
immediately opposite the end of the street. [St Edward's Passage].*

*On the soundtrack : brief snatch of swelling music of
'Somewhere over the Rainbow'.*

*The rain stops instantly. The sun bursts through. Hint of a rainbow.
Still some low black rain clouds, all vividly CGI-enhanced.*

> CHRISSIE
> *(pronounced artificial Italian-American accent:)*
> Gee, that's *gotta* be a wholla *lotta* mora like it!

*She starts to stroll jauntily down King's Parade, the umbrella now
further folded as a small hand-held microphone into which she speaks
rapidly to herself, in a mock dramatic-travelogue and very 'British'
American voice (Peter Sellers, 'Balham Gateway to the South'):*

> And before us we see the splendid shining
> edifice of the King's College Methodist
> Chapel, in the University of Cambridge, the
> United Kingdoms of England and Great
> Britain. For nearly two thousand years, its
> exceptionally unique stained glass windows
> have refuted the ravages of time, ravishing
> the rapt reverence of every ardent admirer

for more than three generations. As we
pass its ancient portals—

*[CGI] Two F16 fighter planes suddenly shoot out of the dark low
cloud and roar past at just above chapel roof level, deafeningly loud.*

*Whole street stops in open-mouthed amazement, horror, outrage.*

*From the direction of the chapel, the unmistakeable and loud sound of
breaking glass.*

                    CHRISSIE
           WOOOoops!!

*A score of people on the street reach angrily for their mobile phones.*


5. INT. COCKPIT OF PLANE. SOARING INTO SKY.

*PILOT 1 is shaken as he sees what he has just nearly hit.
All voices are very urgent & very American—& very redacted:*

                    PILOT 1
           Jeeepuss Christmas! Where'd in darnation did
           that come from!  Alpha-One to Alpha-Base:
           Still in close pursuit. Repeat: no visual contact.

                    INTERCOM
           Alpha Base to Alpha-One. Radar still tracking.
           Keep in pursuit. Report on contact.

                    PILOT 2 VOICE
           Alpha-Two to Alpha-Base:
           confirm no visual contact.

                    BASE
           Alpha-Base to Alpha-One. Radar contact lost.
           Repeat radar contact lost.

VOICE *interrupts*:
Angry Base Commander to Idiot Alpha-One.
What the F— *[bleeped]* Bushmills are you doing
over Cambridge! My ears just got burned off.
Every darn phone on the base is ringing. Break off
pursuit. Repeat: break off pursuit. Report direct to
me. Immediate debriefing. Suffering F — *[bleeped]*
F — *[bleeped]* Crickets Almighty!

## 6. EXT. CLOUDS AND SKY.

*As if the view from a cockpit, soaring up into clear blue skies.
Then fluffy white clouds galore. [Studio Canal Plus.]*

SCROLLING TITLE(S) *[in suitable fonts and formattings]*:

WWW
THE WEEKEND THAT WARPED THE WORLD
GLOBAL WARPING
OCTOBER II : THE SEQUEL
MORPH 8

CREDITS & MUSIC *(semi-Twilight Zone) over blue skies and nice
fluffy clouds, which, as the credits end, become a close-up of Windows-
type screen wallpaper on a computer monitor.*

## 7. INT. AIR TRAFFICE CONTROL ROOM, STANSTED AIRPORT.

*Close-up of digital clouds on a computer monitor.
Loop-scrolling across the screen as a screen-saver :*

Terminal Radar Approach Control London
Stansted Airport Terminal Radar Approach . .

*Menu-bar digital time blinks on the computer screen: 11.10 a.m.*

*Voices-over of routine air-traffic control instructions.*

CONTROLLER ONE *suddenly shouts:*
They're back!

*Pull back to reveal busy radar control room.*
*Urgent 'Collision Alert Procedures' go into operation as all radar*
*screens suddenly show (close-up) several blips in a curious formation.*
*The blips are not moving but are clearly in the path of incoming*
*aircraft. [The formation is a Smiley made up of several dots.]*

*Coolly controlled very calm attempts to avert crashes between incoming*
*aircraft and the mystery blips, as very stiff-upper-lip World War II*
*RAF voices give rapid techno-directional instructions to incoming pilots.*

*Suddenly all the screens show that the blips have disappeared*
*as quickly as they came.*

*CU: Computer menu-bar time reads: '11.15 : Tea-Break'.*

*Pleasant 1940s dance music begins on the room speakers.*
*Everybody in the room reaches for a bone-china cup of tea*
*from a tea-set on each desk, and puts their feet up.*

*As they sip their tea, stir sugar, select cakes, etc, a languid discussion*
*among the slightly elderly and very 'Brit' controllers on the various*
*options for reporting the incident:*

CONTROLLER ONE
Jolly intriguing, what. Second bally time in sixty
bally minutes.

CONTROLLER TWO
45 minutes actually, Number One. According to the
dodgy flight dossier. You still want to report
"enemy aircraft"? — Again?

CONTROLLER THREE
What enemy? War's over, old bean. Well, *our* war is.

CONTROLLER ONE
Ah no, a jolly good war never ends, old son.
Enemy aircraft it is, then. Let's blame the damn
Yankees — Again.

CONTROLLER FOUR *(supercilious lisp)*
Seems Sounder Sense than Number Two's Simply
Silly "EU-FO sightings" — Again.

CONTROLLER FIVE
Personally prefer "phantom phenomena" frankly.

CONTROLLER THREE
Phantom Fourteens, more like, from those
NATO exercises. North by North-West trajectory.

CONTROLLER FOUR *(hurt tone)*
What, the NATO North Sea manoeuvres?
They'd have told us, surely.

PLAINTIVE INTERCOM
Flight AD-007. Has everyone forgotten me?

CONTROLLER TWO
Cripes. Er. Just a mo. *(gulps tea down)*
Runway Two. Cleared to land. What-ho.

PLAINTIVE INTERCOM
*(pause)* —Whaaaat!

CONTROLLER ONE *(suave)*
Terribly sorry old chap. Try Runway One.
Tea-break's over, lads.

*Standard intercom instructions to pilots resume.*

8. FULL SCREEN

*Resumed intercom traffic control voices overlap into the sound of
pounding heavy metal music as a slow visual dissolve into:*

*Close-up of a strange pattern of stationary lights showing against
a deep black background. A smooth pull-back gradually reveals:*

*The image is now Europe at night from satellite distance.
Lights are those of cities and towns, coastlines and major arteries.
Cloud-like vapour whisps drift across it. [Powell & Pressburger]
A sudden piercing whistle..*

*Pull back further. It is the well-known poster-picture of the lights of
Europe at night stuck on the wall of a room.
It is steam from a boiling kettle which is drifting across the picture.
Whistle is the kettle boiling.*

9. INT. FRANK'S ROOM. CONTINUOUS.

*Pull back from wall poster to show:
FRANK reaches out for the whistling kettle and starts to make
instant coffee in a 'UFOs Rule OK' mug.*

*Frank is 18, permanently confined to either bed or his enormous and
very hi-tech wheelchair. Has a long-standing motor-neurone illness.
He lives on the net, his mobile phone, and any other communications
device he can lay his hands on. His ground-floor room is a clutter of
sophisticated electronic gear.*

*He is at one of several computers, while also monitoring Stansted flight
control on some impressive short-wave radio gear, and has been listening
to the urgent evasion instructions from the previous scene.*

*Frank looks excited. He dictates (using voice recognition)
an e-mail to friend ALEX. We see the text on screen:
the date/time on the email is 10.10.11.17 a.m.*

> FRANK *(dictating)*
> Email: To Alex: Begin: 'Hi Alex.
> Something VERY hot been happening
> over Stansted and Cambridge.
> Seems to be major sightings! Radar
> confirmation too. Come round this
> evening if you can. Frank.' End. Send.

*Frank goes back to monitoring different channels. He also has several websites up on his various computer screens, all to do with UFOs and similar. And loud rock music is playing on a major sound system.*

*Abruptly all sound cuts out, to an eerie whispering quiet, as:*

## 10. INT. DARK ROOM.

*A FIGURE is silhouetted against a large window.*
*Only black outline visible: a large round head on a tall slim body.*

*A green-gloved hand turns a dial. A monitor blinks into action, showing SIR GEE-GEE on a video-link.*

> FIGURE
> *(female voice, very odd accent)*
> This is getting out of hand.
> We need a cover story.
> Some distractions.

> GEE-GEE
> Give me an hour to set something up.

> FIGURE
> I can lend you two excellent agents.

> GEE-GEE
> Fine. And I'll reactivate the old team.

> FIGURE
> Remember, the last thing we want
> is the truth, anywhere out there.
> Just weave a tangled web, or two.

## 11. INT. SITTING ROOM. EVENING.

WRITTEN:
> CAMBRIDGE (UK, OK?),
> THE SITTING ROOM,
> 6.27 P.M.

*BRIAN WINSTON, aged 36, is watching the end of the local evening television news with his son, ALEX, aged 15. Comfortable but untidy middle class home.*

> NEWS ANNOUNCER ON TV
> . . so at the close of play the England team are again in deep trouble. *[Pause]*
> And finally, an unexpected sight over the city of Cambridge this morning—.

*On the TV screen, some wobbly amateur video footage barely shows the streak of two passing aircraft over King's Parade.*

> REPORTER VOICE-OVER
> Two fighter planes from an aircraft carrier taking part in secret NATO exercises in the North Sea came close to destroying one of the country's finest tourist attractions today. A military spokesperson said that initial investigations clearly indicated a probable unexplained error. A university spokesperson has so far declined to comment—.

> BRIAN
> *(switches TV sound off with the remote)*
> That means they couldn't find anybody from the university awake enough at ten in the morning to have seen it. OK, Alex, homework.

*The TV is now showing, silently, a short weather forecast for the East Anglia region. The curving outline of the Norfolk, Suffolk and Essex coastline is visible.*

> ALEX
> It's the weekend, Dad. Thank God it's Friday. No homework due till Monday.

> BRIAN
> It's Friday? Again? Already? Forgot.
> OK, dinner in one hour.

ALEX
Fish and chips again?

BRIAN
Neither of us has time, talent or inclination to cook.
Prefer a curry? Again?

ALEX
Yup. Momtaz?

BRIAN
One hour. I've got work to do if you haven't.

*The TV is now showing brief trailer-clips for a weekend of sci-fi films:
Earth versus the Flying Saucers, Them, It Came From Outer Space,
and The Blob. Brian watches briefly, then switches off.*

*They go to their own rooms in the big detached house.*

## 12. INT. BRIAN'S STUDY. *[brief scene]*

*Brian enters a ground floor home office with an impressive array of
several computers and related equipment. He switches on two radios
simultaneously: a hideous mix of pseudo-Ornette Coleman avant-garde
jazz and pseudo-Jimi Hendrix. The computers show a screen logo:
WC SS : Winston Computer Security Systems. Brian settles to work.*

## 13. INT. ALEX'S BEDROOM.

*Alex enters an upstairs bedroom, with one impressive computer,
with a very large graphics monitor, a scanner, with a removeable USB
wireless connector. Boots up his computer; it plays quiet Bach music.*

*Both Brian's and Alex's rooms have the same framed photo of their
dead wife / mother somewhere very visible in the room.*

*Alex logs on, reads (out) the e-mail from Frank.
Types reply. We see his reply on screen:*

'OK. I'll come round about 9 if Dad'll let me.
Alex.'

*Alex clicks on his browser Favourites menu.*
*Brings up a screenful of dozens of thumb-nail images of female nudes.*
*They appear at first to be from some very soft porn site.*

*The Camera zooms rapidly in to get a much closer look.*
*It blurs out of focus. Recovers.*

*CU: The nudes are recognisably famous paintings from*
*an image bank of art works from the National Gallery, London.*
*The web-page displays the prominent logo of SoftCorps Inc.*

## 14. EXT. MOMTAZ CURRY HOUSE. EVENING.

*Echo the opening shot, but now a fast tilt (to jaunty Indian pop music)*
*up bright flashing fairy-lit & over-the-top window decorations of*
*'MOMTAZ Curry House'. Finish on the lighted sign above window:*
*'MOMTAZ'—but the light is defunct on the Z, so 'MOMTA-'.*

WRITTEN:

MOMTA-  Curry House,
7.46 pm.
*[the time changes to 7.47 even as we watch.]*

## 15. INT. MOMTAZ CURRY HOUSE. EVENING.
*(brightly awful Indian music)*

*Brian and Alex are seated  at a table against the wall.*
*Waiter VENKAT comes over with Menu. He knows them well.*

BRIAN

Evening, Venkat.

VENKAT

Need I ask?

*Brian and Alex nod. Venkat leaves, with unused menu.*

*Chrissie barges into the restaurant and though the place
is mainly empty she squeezes herself onto their table.
They do not know her. She is now a red-head.
She unfurls her umbrella-laptop and plugs it into a wall socket near
their table. She pivots the now tablet computer into a touch-screen
keyboard mode. Begins tapping away.*

> BRIAN
> *(at the laptop:)*
> Wow!!

> CHRISSIE
> Bless you. *(in pronounced artificial and very prim Scottish
> [Maggie Smith] accent, introduces herself while still working:)*
> Christine McTavish MacDougall Flaherty O'Brian.
> Guid evening. Ah hope ye dinna mind mah seating
> here, but this is absoloo-telly the only table with a
> convenient electrical-type socket. Which Ah need
> for mah work. So Ah eat here everrry evening. Do
> ignore me. Ye may go elsewhere if Ah bother you.
> Ah will not be offended, Ah do assure ye.

*Alex is impressed by Chrissie. Brian is impressed by the laptop.
Both are amused rather than irritated.*

> BRIAN
> Not at all. We eat here quite often too, in fact.
> But I haven't seen you here before. My name's
> Brian, my son Alex. I do admire your lap—

*Interrupted by his mobile phone ringing. As he fishes for it, continues
lamely:*

> —top. I mean. Lap-top. Sorry, excuse me.
> *(listens, then into phone)* Right now? Sure.
> Be right round. *(to Alex)* Sorry, son.
> Sir Gee-Gee calls. Something pretty urgent.
> I'll eat there. Scoff what you can. *(about to
> leave quickly, remembers.)* Here, take a tenner.
> Should cover it. *(Alex looks quizzical.)*
> OK, another. *(hands Alex two £10 notes).*

ALEX

Can I still go to Frank's?

BRIAN

Er yes, but be in by ten. Or you're grounded.
You know the rules of the game. *Au Renoir.*

*Venkat arrives with large meal. Includes a Coke and a lager.*

VENKAT

Two Usuals.

*Brian dashes out of restaurant*

VENKAT

*(Resignedly, to Alex.)* They normally eat the stuff
*before* leaving without paying. Hope you're hungry.
But you're too young for this, my son.
*(Drinks the lager in one gulp.)*

*Venkat piles several full dishes onto the table and leaves.*
*The meal is far too much for Alex alone.*

ALEX

*(to Chrissie, hesitantly, almost a pick-up:)*
Erm, if you're eating as well as working, would you
like to join me? There's too much for me here.
My Dad's gone to Jesus.

CHRISSIE

*(amused at the phrase.)* Seems rather sudden.

ALEX

Sorry, I meant he's gone to Jesus College.
Round the corner. For dinner. Sudden invitation.
From Sir Gee-Gee.

CHRISSIE

A horse? That I could eat. *(Yiddish intonation.)*

ALEX
No, Sir Gerald Gregory-Graham.
He's one of my Dad's clients. I think.

CHRISSIE
*(Looks a little warily at him, then at the food.*
*Then, in US John Wayne Western mode: )*
Don't mind if I do, pardner. Pass the beans.

*They start to eat but Chrissie doesn't switch off her laptop.*
*Alex tries to make conversation.*

ALEX
Help yourself. Er, what are you working on?

CHRISSIE
*(clipped robotic data voice, between bites: )*
First year Computer Science student. Arrived.
Two days ago. First lecture. This morning.
Missed it. Downloading it. From net. University
puts lectures on net. For students. Like me.
On neural nets. Introduction to. Already know.
About. Neural nets.

ALEX
I see. *(pause)* What's a neural net?

CHRISSIE
*(in ingratiating German professorial accent:)*
Vell now, ze neural net iz an entirely interezting
phaenomenon, not entirely underztood—

*She digs into the rice. Camera zooms into an extreme close-up*
*of not very appetising Indian curry. Indian music fades.*

POLITELY SELF-EFFACING VOICE-OVER
*(very BBC)*:
For more information on neural nets, interactive
viewers may now press the blue velvet button.

*A white button appears in top left corner of the screen.*
*A twisted  disembodied arthritic finger materialises and presses it.*
*Twice.  Nothing happens.*

> POLITELY PATRONISING VOICE-OVER:
> No, dear. The *Blue* button.

*Finger gives exceedingly impolite gesture & disappears. Button fades.*
*Cross-fade to close-up of spotless table laid for a sumptuous meal:*

## 16. INT. HIGH TABLE. JESUS COLLEGE.

*Distant and beautiful soundtrack: a boy soprano singing*
*"Now let thy servant depart in peace" [the Tinker Tailor version], as:*

*Pull back to show the High Table at Jesus College.*
*The boy chorister is singing near the High Table.*

WRITTEN:
> HIGH TABLE
> 20.01 P.M.
> SOUP COURSE.

*Brian and SIR GERALD GREGORY-GRAHAM*
*(Sir Gee-Gee) are seated together, sipping soup. A few other dons at*
*the high table, totally absorbed in food or fast asleep. One has a bib.*

*Sir Gee-Gee is (apparently) a retired senior intelligence officer.*
*Now got a cushy number as (Deputy) Master of the College.*
*The following is very Alec Guiness (Smiley), nonchalant-confidential.*
*GG gestures to halt the singing, and dismisses the chorister.*

> GG
> Boy sopranos. Can't beat 'em, y'know, Brian.
> Brings tears to the eyes. Against the law, though.
> Pity.
>> BRIAN
>> Er, not my type, Sir Gerald. Of music, I mean.

GG

Any rate, so glad you could come.
Got a little job for you. You heard about
that *fracas* over King's this morning.

BRIAN

Well, I heard some priceless windows were
smashed.

GG

Good Lord, no. People do jump to conclusions.
Some dozy blighter walked into a stack of empty
wine bottles outside the college kitchens.
Looking up at those damn planes. Dreadful noise.
But no real damage. The University's a bit
concerned, though. Asked me to investigate.
On the quiet.

BRIAN

What, the broken bottles?

GG

Of course not, dear boy. Why those planes
were so completely off-course. Blighters.
Should have been somewhere over Lakenheath.

BRIAN

The old US airbase? Why?

GG

Well, seems there were some rather odd reports.
Y'know. Radar blips. Stansted caught them too.
Strange patterns. Unidentified whatnots. The usual.
Croutons. (*asking Brian to pass croutons for the soup:*)
Soup alright? It's duck, I believe.

*A liveried waiter comes to clear their plates and serve the next course.
GG ostentatiously puts his finger to his lips to hush Brian.*

17. INT. CURRY HOUSE.

*The debris of the meal is growing. Chrissie is still half-working on her laptop while eating and talking.*

> CHRISSIE
> *(finally finishing a long explanation.)*
> Zo, now you underztand ze neural netz, Ja?

> ALEX *(amused)*
> Not in the slightest. My Dad's more into this stuff than I am. He used to teach computing.
> But then he set up as a freelance security consultant, anti-hacking, that sort of thing.

> CHRISSIE
> *(conspiratorial voice, vaguely French:)*
> Zen 'e vould not happrove hof me.
> Chretienne Dreyfuss-Poirot, 'Acker Extraordinaire.
> I vill now 'ack into dis mouton curie.

> VENKAT *comes over.*
> Your bill. Sir. Just in case.

> CHRISSIE
> Does he get my discount?

> VENKAT
> Ah, no, no, Contessa.

18. INT. HIGH TABLE. JESUS COLLEGE.
WRITTEN:
> 20:14. Coarse Fish.

*The fish course is being served. Several dishes.*
*A Barber's Shop quartet is now visible in the background and is harmoniously singing a round version of 'The Lobster Quadrille'.*
*— add your own choice of fish-related musical alternatives ad libitum.*

BRIAN

But why rope me in, Sir Gee-Gee?
I haven't been in the service for several years now.


GG

Ah, yes, the good old slimey days. Enjoyed them.
Look, Brian, I want an outsider view on this one.
MI7.5 have assigned Harry Cotter. Nothing against
Cotter personally, of course. Damn fine officer.
But a totally incompetent cretin. Convinced there's
a secret terrorist cell behind every minor incident.
Can never see anything except the usual suspects.
Moles. Sleepers. Oysters? *(offering dish)* And the
Americans have muscled in as well. Assigned us
some woman called Carol Lewis as liaison.
Dangerous fantasist. Thinks we're always dealing
with alien invasion threats. I've nothing against
women, of course. As you know. Just can't stand
Yanks. So I want you to offer a sane alternative.
Those F16s could have gone off course for a whole
variety of reasons, nothing to do with sabotage.
Your kind of field, I suspect. Viruses. Bugs. Pranks.
Prawns? They're quite good.


BRIAN

Er, yes. Thank you. *(takes some fish)*
Well, it could have been a bug in the navigation
software. Or a defective GPS device.


GG

GPS?


*A flashing white button appears at the top right of the screen—
the old reel-change signal. A hopeful Finger appears. Button vanishes.
The Finger fades. A slight 'reel-change' jump-cut in the visual track.*


BRIAN

GPS, GG, is a form of GSP-GG.
A Geostationary Positioned Satellite Guidance
Gadget. Got it? But that wouldn't explain the

Stansted blips. By itself, that too could have been just a virus. Or a hacker attacker. But a combination of the two stretches it a bit. *(laughs)* You never know, it might even have been an actual UFO!

                              GG
Well, keep an open mind. Not too open, mind. You know how the service operates. We need a credible civilian front on this—and you still have security clearance. So we can always disown you, slander you, or arrest you, if necessary.
The University doesn't want fighter planes, let alone little green men, frightening the tourists on King's Parade. But if it's left to MI7.5 it'd be an Official Secret even if Venusians landed on the lawn. So I said I'd make some discreet inquiries. You're my discreet inquirer—and I'm sure you'll find Damien's little lamb quite delicious. *(explains:)* The college chef's speciality. The main course.

## 19. INT. HETI OPERATIONS ROOM.
WRITTEN:

H.E.T.I. : 20.01- 22.05 P.M.

[*then in even smaller lettering:*

For information on HETI just press any red button.
Or be patient for once and wait a minute. OK?]

*HETI is a pretty amateur set-up, with ageing monitors and other equipment. Some ancient Amigas and Ataris are visible, mainly showing old games in progress. One wall screen is showing a Hubble-type image of distant galaxies, but with some stars oddly flashing on and off, creating a series of patterns that (not too obviously) echo the Smiley pattern of the Stansted episode.*

*Male Assistant Two is playing Sudoku, barely looking at the screen. Female Assistant One appears, with two grimy mugs of tea in "UFOs For Real Madrid" mugs. She sees the wall screen image.*

ASSISTANT ONE *(very excited)*
How long's that flashing been going on?

ASSISTANT TWO *(indifferent)*
Who, me? —Oh, the screen. Hours.
Bloody monitor's on the blink, I suppose.

ASSISTANT ONE *(very very excited)*
But aren't they brand new stars?

ASSISTANT TWO *(bored yawn)*
Who cares. A star is born every bleeding minute.
Remember we're looking for celestial *Coronation
Street*, eternal *East Enders*, not *Starlight Express*.

20. INT. CURRY HOUSE.

*Several empty ice cream bowls on the table.*
*Chrissie is still working at laptop. Ignoring Alex.*

*[Overlaid Speed-Dating set-up: On-screen scores track the following
exchanges, while very small persons in lower corners of the screen,
one for each speaker, give rapid but random Sign Language gestures:]*

ALEX *(hopelessly over-tentative..)*
Er, you'd get on well with my friend Frank.
He's never off the net, either. A real computer
freak. Erm. I'm supposed to go round and see him
tonight. Erm. Would you like to meet him?

*[very low scores come up on the screen…animated figures show
contempt]*

CHRISSIE *(bargaining tone)*
Is he tall, dark, handsome, with a private income,
a private jet, a cottage in the Caribbean, huge assets,
and, most important, does he have a room to rent?

ALEX

Well, I'm afraid Frank is actually, er, height-
challenged and weight-challenged, and lives on a
tiny disability allowance. He's been in a wheelchair
since he was a kid. Motor neurone. That's why he
sort of lives on the web. Why do you need a room?

CHRISSIE

Long Term Investment Opportunity, of course.
*(her own voice, finally)* Look, I thought I'd go
independent, living away from home for the first
time. So, daft bugger, I turned down a college room
and found myself cheap digs upstairs *here*.
*(scornful laugh.)*

VENKAT
*(in background) (scornful laugh)*

*[Briefly, there are three fast-dating score judges on the screen,
all laughing scornfully —in Sign Language.]*

CHRISSIE

At least I get a discount on meals in the restaurant.
But otherwise the room is bleeped [*bleep*] awful.
So I'm looking for somewhere else. Fast. OK?
*[golden opportunity opening move for him—]*

ALEX

Erm, *we* have a room to rent.
*[blows it: too fast & too nervous: a minus score :]*
My mum died ten years ago. Air accident.
Caused by a bug in the autopilot software.
That's why my Dad moved into that field.
But we kept the house on and it's really too big for
just the two of us. So we sometimes rent out a
room. So, erm, come and meet Frank, then maybe,
erm, come home and, erm, look at the room?? Erm.

*[His on-screeen score has plummetted. His Figure shakes its head sadly.]*

*Chrissie looks pityingly at this pathetic performance.*
*She decides that Alex's pulling routine poses no serious threat, or*
*promise. Folds up the laptop into umbrella mode.*

> CHRISSIE
> OK. Let's go see Frank. Have you paid?
> You can leave my discount as a tip if you like.

> ALEX
> Eh? Not sure I follow that. *(looks at bill)* But we've
> got just enough change for a taxi—it's pouring
> again.

*[On-screen Figures put up umbrellas and leave together, arm in arm.]*


## 21. EXT. FRANK'S HOUSE.

*Taxi arrives with Alex and Chrissie. It is now a dark, wet and windy*
*night. Horror movie moonlight. Trees swaying over a short driveway to*
*a spooky and gloomy house. Elm Street type. The name-plate is split*
*across the double gate: 'Elms —Tree'.*

*As Alex and Chrissie get out of the taxi, we hear loud horror movie*
*music mounting on the soundtrack. Then a spine-tingling scream from*
*the house. The Taxi driver looks horrified. Alex pays him.*

> ALEX
> Let me give you a tip, Taxi Driver.

*A second scream. Taxi screeches off at high speed, without waiting for*
*the tip.*

> ALEX
> *(shouts after departing taxi:)*
> Get your back-seat cleaned. It's all sticky.

*They dash through the driving rain to the front door, under the pink*
*(laptop-)umbrella. Alex distracted by something sticky on his trouser*
*seat. Chrissie giggles slightly at this.*

*The music and horrible screams continue. Alex more concerned about his trousers. He rings doorbell. Music and screams still continue. Chrissie is amused.*

*The name plate on door is : 'Pine Wood'. Alex rings the bell again. Music and screaming abruptly stop in mid-bar/ howl. Pause until :*

*Mad-looking woman, MAGDA DICKSON, comes to the door, framed in a lurid green security light, dishevelled, with hair standing on end, and wide-staring eyes. She recognises Alex. Shakes out of her mood. In a beautifully calm, pleasant, and cultured voice:*

> MAGDA
> Ah, good evening Alex. Frank's been expecting you. Sorry I didn't hear the bell. I've been trying to finish a soundtrack.

> ALEX
> Horror?

> MAGDA
> Indeed, yes. Perfectly dreadful movie. *Californica Screamer VI.* Sort of Frankenstein meets Al Capone meets Deep Throat. Political horror thriller gangster comedy. Real pain. Do come in. And this is?

> ALEX
> *(realises he doesn't know her real name)* Erm.

> MAGA
> Well, hello Erm.

*[There is an audible groan on the soundtrack. Magda hears it but ignores it.]*

> CHRISSIE *(very Northern Irish accent)*
> Chrissie MacMahon Fingal O'Flaherty Yeats Wilde.

> MAGDA
> As in Oscar?

CHRISSIE *(simpering Hollywood)*
I'd be really glad to hope so, ma'am.

MAGDA
I'm Magda. Or Anna. Or Lena. As you prefer.

CHRISSIE
As in Bach Chronicle?

MAGDA
Indeed. Well, go into Frank. I'll bring you all
some coke. Or sponsored coffee? Or bitter tea?

*She bustles off in the direction of the kitchen.*
*Alex leads Chrissie through the house towards Frank's room,*
*passing Magda's work-room with very sophisticated recording set-up,*
*multi-voice electronic keyboard and computer.*

*Paused on a huge TV screen is an extremely lurid scene from the movie*
*she is working on, with a large XXX across it and 'Your Eyes Only'.*

ALEX
That's Frank's mother. She writes film scores.
Somebody has to, I suppose. His Dad's a TV
journalist, Reginald Dixon, always seems to be
somewhere exotic, covering wars and disasters.
Frank's the sane one.

22. INT. FRANK'S GROUND FLOOR ROOM..

*Frank is surrounded by empty coffee mugs and coke tins. Is very excited*
*indeed. Hardly sane. Nearly chokes on an old cold coffee as they enter.*

FRANK
Yuk! No, great! Right. Glad you came. Things are
moving! This may be the Big One. I think they're
really THERE. Or even HERE!! Who's this?

ALEX
Chrissie, Frank. Frank, Chrissie.
Who's here? Or there?

CHRISSIE
*(Australian accent, holding out her hand in a hearty
handshake:)* Pleased ta meet ya Frank. Put it there.

ALEX
She's from Earl's Court. I think.
Now, what's got you so excited?

FRANK
I think THEY have finally made CONTACT.
At last. Well, nearly so. Maybe. Look at this latest
stuff from HETI. Fantastico!

*Points to his largest monitor, showing a live website from HETI with
the flashing galaxies image.*

CHRISSIE
Who's Hettie?

FRANK
HETI. —H-E-T-I is the British equivalent of SETI,
Search for Extraterrestrial Intelligence.

ALEX
Except that we Brits can't actually afford to *search*
for anything, so HET stands for 'Hope for
Extraterrestrial' —and HETI thinks we'll probably
get a visual signal rather than a radio message, so it's
'Hope for Extra-Terrestrial *Images*.'

FRANK
We've been pumping crap TV out into space for
decades, so maybe 'They' have too. So HETI looks
for ET's *East-Enders* rather than the solution to
American Pi. Alien *Big Brother*, not alien super
intelligence.

ALEX

HETI's just down the road from here.
At Madingley. Near the old Radio Telescope.
But they can't afford high-spec receivers of their
own. So they scour people's image data-bases
to see if there's anything odd. Checking out Hubble
data for weird signal patterns. That kind of stuff.

FRANK

And they've finally struck gold! Look now!
I started logging this at eight o'clock this evening.
And if that's not a message, what is?

*Triumphantly points to a screen. The HETI website. By now, the Hubble-type image's remote stars are not only blinking on and off but also constantly re-arranging themselves into changing patterns.*

FRANK

Been going on all evening. And they're NEW stars.
If they *are* stars. Might be something quite awesome.
Mother ships the size of stars. Moving in formation.
And getting closer. Incredibly fast. It's the only
explanation.

CHRISSIE
*(quietly sings)* Wee free stars…

FRANK

There was a huge panic flap over Stansted this
morning. I'm sure the military were tracking *real*
UFOs. They might even have landed. Sent us this
message and then arrived. *Pronto.* First Class mail.

CHRISSIE

So that's what those fighter-planes were chasing
over Cambridge this morning? Aliens travelled
several million light years to make me miss a lecture.
Bloody typical.

MAGDA
*(appears with coffees)* Coffee anyone?

*Chrissie takes one and sips. Nearly chokes.*

CHRISSIE
Truly delightful coffee, Ma'am.

23. INT. SENIOR COMMON ROOM.
WRITTEN:
S.C.R. 9.59.
AND SO TO PORT.

*Brian and GG are now having port and excellent coffee in the Senior Common Room. Audible but not visible is an entire choir singing Bach's 'Schweigt stille, plaudert nicht ' ('Be still, stop chattering' — The Coffee Cantata : BWV 211)*

BRIAN
Truly delightful coffee, Sir GeeGee. What brand?

*GG hands Brian two DVDs, explaining:*

GG
OK Brian, take that, and then this. Analyse this first. All the screen shots and radar data from Stansted. Then analyse that. The flight paths and cockpit data from the F16s. Highly hush-hush, of course. Cotter will bring any updates around tomorrow. About 11 if that suits. Put together a preliminary analysis over the weekend.
And do pass the port, please. The right way.

BRIAN
Right, Geegee. *(passes the port)*. Look, I've got to go. *(looks at watch)* My son should be home by now. *(pause)* Damn good coffee, though. And *porto e bello*, eh? *(reaches for the port)*

GG
One for the old Kent road, then?

*Sudden screech of music as cut to CU of very old-fashioned gramophone playing a stuck vynil record of the Bach piece.*


24. INT. FRANK'S ROOM.

ALEX
Look, I've got to go. (*looks at watch*) My Dad should be home by now. Aliens landing or not, Frank, I'm going to be grounded if I'm not in by ten. (*explains to Chrissie:*) My Dad grounds me by taking away my net access. I'm stuck in off-line mode till I get it back. Real pain.

FRANK
(*to Chrissie:*) Glad we met. I'm fd1 at freimail dot com. Keep in touch.

CHRISSIE
(*pats her umbrella-laptop*) And this is Erika at Aye Eye dot com. With me at all times. Never grounded.

FRANK (*puzzled*)
Aye Eye? 'A.Y.E. E.Y.E.' The software company? Artificial Intelligence development. Neural net research?

CHRISSIE
Yup. That's the one. My big sister started the company. Now she wants me to follow in her feetstops. Erika was a present from her. (*unfurls the beautiful sleek computer from the pink umbrella-handle.*)

FRANK
*Very* Cool.

CHRISSIE
It's a neural net machine. Prototype. Emulates any
operating system. Highly intelligent. Very versatile.
Runs pretty well any software you can throw at it.

FRANK
Awesome. Out of this world!

CHRISSIE
Not quite. *And* it's an umbrella.

ALEX
Very handy too. But we gotta go. No taxi either.
Do you still want to see that room?

CHRISSIE
Too late now. But I'll call by tomorrow.
About eleven?

ALEX
I'll walk you home then? Erm, I have to go
that way anyway.

CHRISSIE
*(BBC Jane Austen voice.)*
I shall accept your gracious accompaniment with
pleasure, gallant sir, if a trifle warily. I have your
reputation to consider, after all. *(Japanese voice and
bow, to Frank:)* Farewell-greetings, Francisco-San.

25. EXT. KING'S BACKS.
WRITTEN:
THE BACHS. 21.59 P.M.

*It is now a lovely moonlit night. Alex is walking Chrissie home.
He is very unsure of himself. She is amused by his embarrassed
presumption. King's College Chapel is visible in the moonlight behind
them. The sound of polyphonic romantic Madrigals gently audible.*

ALEX

That must be the King's choir rehearsing.
You wouldn't think they'd be at it this late.
Monteverdi or Gabrieli, I think.

CHRISSIE

Indeed? More friends of yours?

ALEX

Er, no. 16th century Venetian composers.

*Suddenly a very strong vertical light hits King's Chapel from unseen source above. [clearly CGI] They do not notice. But a sudden wrong note causes a total musical collapse. The strange Light goes off.*

CHRISSIE

Sounds like they gotta problem Houston.
Is that your main interest? Music?

ALEX

Actually, no. It's art history. But I'll be doing art
and music A-levels soon. That's all I really use
computers for, I'm afraid.

CHRISSIE

Mmm. Art history. Well, I might have something
that would interest you. I'll show you tomorrow.
Now, thanks, but I know where I'm going now.
And I can hear distant thunder. And summer
lightning. So bye-ee.

*She leaves, putting up the umbrella as she does so. It immediately starts to rain again, very heavily. And the moon instantly goes behind a cloud. The Choir starts singing a mournful Dies Irae.*

26. EXT. POURING RAIN.
[*Dies Irae continues on soundtrack*]

*Soaked, Alex is now trudging back through the pouring rain. He looks at his watch. Is baffled at the time.*

ALEX
It *can't* be that late! Where did all the time go?

27. INT. BRIAN'S ROOM IN HOUSE.
WRITTEN:
HERE AGAIN
23.51 p.m.

*Brian is annoyed, waiting up for Alex. Working on some of GG's DVD data. He is matching screen-grabs showing digital maps from the F16 flight-guidance system with other web-based and hard copy maps of East Anglia, especially the coastline. The desk is littered with maps.*

*He is listening to the radio, from which the closing verse of the* Dies Irae *is audible.*

*It finishes.*

*A quiet but exasperated* RADIO 3 VOICE *says:*

We do apologise for an unfortunate technical hitch earlier in that live broadcast from King's College Cambridge. The performers suddenly claimed to have seen a great light. (*sceptical :*) Well.
Now, we begin a festival of New Brand British Music, specially commisssioned by the BBC in association with El Tesco Avant-Gardia Musica. First, a performance of the 'DIY Cackophoney, for Drill Machine and ChainSaw', by the recently naturalised Tibetan composer, Maurice Van-Flan O'Brien, here conducted by Jerzy 'Wee Willie' Skorenski, with Jean-Luc Picardy on the electric piccolo, and the Nederlandish Concertgeebouw Orkestra, recorded at the Latvian Brass Band Competition Finale last August in New York, Connecticut. The second violinist is English.

*An excruciating cacophony begins. And continues in the background.*

*Meanwhile, Brian is puzzled by what seems to be something awry with the shape of the East Anglia coastline on the F16 data. Follows it with his stylus. What emerges, not too obviously, is that the coastline now seems to trace the outline of a wrinkled old man's face looking out to sea. A 'Profile' shape.*

*Bedraggled Alex enters.*

>                    BRIAN
> It's nearly midnight, cowboy. OK, usual penalty.
> Bring me your USB modem. Digital grounding till
> Sunday evening. No argument. Now, to bed.

>                    ALEX
> Sorry, Dad. But I had to walk Chrissie home.

>                    BRIAN
> *(surprised, amused, intrigued)* I beg your pardon?
> The young lady in the Momtaz? Do tell me more.

>                    ALEX
> She works for Aye Eye. And she's coming round,
> at eleven tomorrow. She wants to rent a room.
> Is that OK?

>                    BRIAN
> AA, eh? Bit young for Alcoholics Anon, isn't she?
> Er, we'll see. Tomorrow. Now, go to bed.
> It's nearly tomorrow already.

>                    ALEX
> Yes, Dad. *(pause)* Er, could I ask you to explain
> something to me?

>                    BRIAN *(looks very wary)*
> I thought you already . . Er, what about, son?

>                    ALEX
> What's a neural net?

> BRIAN *(mightily relieved)*
> I'll tell you tomorrow, son. Now, bed.

> ALEX
> OK, Dad.  Er—would you turn the music down.
> Please.

*As Alex turns to go:*

> BRIAN
> What's that stain on your trousers, Alex?

> ALEX
> The back-seat of the taxi was filthy.

> BRIAN
> Oh?

*Brian turns the radio down as the sound modulates into highly dramatic 'suspense' music over:*


28. EXT. COASTAL WATERS. NIGHT. DENSE FOG.
WRITTEN:
> Ye Suffex Coast.
> 00.01 a.m.

*British World War II movie style editing. Almost black and white. Water reflections, tense faces in foggy dark, etc. The dramatic soundtrack continues, ambiguously, from the BBC radio broadcast.*

*A military landing craft is approaching the coast through very thick fog. Shots of tense personnel on the bridge show that they are navigating only by tracking radar and GPS data on screens, which show the outline of the Suffolk-Essex coast getting closer.*

*This is a multi-national NATO invasion exercise.*

*Grim blacked-up commandos are waiting to leap ashore from the landing ramp. On the bridge the German captain, in a white rollneck sweater and rakish cap, gives grimly unintelligible guttural monosyllabic instructions to the helmsman.*

>                    NAVIGATOR *(Black Cockney)*
> Charlie Tango he say: We hit the beach in thirty
> seconds, precisely, dead reckoning, Mein Kapitan
> Herr Kampf. *(counts rapidly)*. Twenty-five. Twenty.
> Ten. Alpha-ville!

*Troops poised— the landing ramp rattles down.*

>                    SERGEANT *(Japanese)*
> G0, *GO*, **GO!**

*The fog very suddenly clears, revealing that the coast is still several hundred yards distant.*

>                    SERGEANT
> WOAHHH!!!  VAIT FOR IT!

*Troops fall over each other, Keystone Cops style. Chaos.*

>                    SERGEANT
> Vhat the fog! *[late bleep]*. FOG, I said!

*Captain looks through his night goggles. It dawns that they are several hundred yards away from the coast. Bafflement.*

*Rapid simultaneous execrations in Euro-Lingua re baffling situation. With violent gestures at instrument panel readings.*

>                    GERMAN CAPTAIN
> Ver ist der bleeden coaster verlanden?
> Das Boot! Donner und Blitzen! Verfukt der mein
> Vaterland.

FRENCH HELMSMAN
Merd-i gras! L'année derniere a Marienbad! Sans
soleil! Où est la Belle du jour! C'est mystère!
Non bleedin' compris. Et cétera sera.

ITALIAN ADMIRAL
Botticelli-Bolognese! La Dolce Vita. Sei kilometri?
Impossibilé. Ai que-ida no corri-dor?

MATCHING SUBTITLES, WRITTEN:

Blimey, the coastline would appear to have evanesced.

That ist quite amazing. Even so.

One point four miles short taken!

*Add Swedish Bergmanesque subtitles under the English sub-titles.*

*And a European Union logo.*

FADE TO BLACK.

INTERVAL
*(with ice creams)*

*

29. FULL SCREEN BLACK.

*Dramatic music,* still *continuing from Friday's radio broadcast.*

*Slowly fade up from black, to:*

*Close-up of Hubble image with flashing Smiley patterns of stars.*

WRITTEN:
>     FADE UP FROM BLACK / FRIDAY.

*Writing quickly fades to black.*

WRITTEN: TYPED-IN, LETTER BY LETTER:

## S.A.T.U.R.D.A.Y.

*Pull back from Hubble image to show that it is on a large screen in:*

30. INT. HETI HQ. MORNING.

WRITTEN:
*('24 HOURS' mode):*

. . H.E.T.I., MADINGLEY, CANATAB, SATURDAY 11.10, 10.01 A.M ...

*Writing fades to black.*

WRITTEN *(in small print):*

>     Remember?  H.E.T.I. = H.Q. OF BRITISH SETI ?
>     If not, just press the sodding red button.

*Several monitors around the room are showing variations of the Hubble image with patterns of apparently new stars continually appearing.*

*The male Director and female Assistant One are (more or less) straight out of a bad 1950s British SF script or Advertising Scientist mode. White coats, glasses, uptight.*

*Whereas male Assistant Two is a laid-back sceptical no-hoper ageing hippie, out of Dark Star. Dramatic Music pauses.*

> DIRECTOR
> Good Grief! Another new set!
> Have you ever seen anything like this before!

> ASSISTANT TWO
> *(still doing the same Sudoku puzzle as in scene 19)*
> Yup. Yesterday. Told you, but you wouldn't
> sodding listen

> ASSISTANT ONE
> Yes, Director, sir. We've had sixty-nine different
> sets of new star positions since yesterday.
> It's clearly not a natural phenomenon.
> They seem to *mean* something.

*Medium loud crescendo of Dramatic Music.*

> DIRECTOR
> Yes! But what do they *mean*?

> ASSISTANT TWO
> They mean bleedin' overtime. On a Saturday.
> Blue meanies. I've been up all bleepin' night.

> ASSISTANT ONE
> Remember, Herr Direktor sir, we only have visual
> sightings. They're not confirmed by any other data.

> DIRECTOR
> Yes, Assistant One, but they appear to be over a
> thousand light years away, so if this is a message
> it must have been sent a thousand years ago.
> What's it *telling* us??

*Medium quiet crescendo of semi-Dramatic music.*

ASSISTANT TWO

The result of the Battle of Hastings? One Nil.
Has it occurred to you, Sir Director Herr sir,
that it might just be the visual data that are
changing, not new stars actually forming
before our very eyes. That is, a thousand years
before our very eyes.

ASSISTANT ONE

But, Herr Sir Director, we've checked and re-
checked. The data is definitely there.

ASSISTANT TWO

*Data ARE* definitely there, don't you mean?
It's a sodding plural, dammit. But where is there?
There's no *there* in data-space. (b*rief loud music chord.*)
And can we have that damn radio OFF!

DIRECTOR

You mean: whoever is sending this data isn't
actually a thousand light years away. But a lot closer.

*Crescendo of Very Dramatic music on soundtrack.*

ASSISTANT ONE

You mean, you think they could be a lot closer
than we think.

DIRECTOR

What do you think?

*Identical music crescendo again.*

ASSISTANT TWO

I think you're *not* thinking. *I* think it's just our
image-processing software screwing up.
We got it from the Beta-Ware catalogue after all.
And you're not *listening* either. Can we turn that
damn *radio* OFF.

DIRECTOR

Look, I'm making an executive decision. Right now.
I know some of you will find this difficult. But I'm
imposing a complete silence ban on this data.
Nobody is to know about it, er, them, even inside
this room. And we certainly won't put these, this,
data up on the web-site any longer. Until we're
sure. It would only cause a panic. And we don't
want that. Yet.

ASSISTANT ONE

Surely we might let the government know, herr sir.
They wouldn't panic. Would they?

ASSISTANT TWO

It's Saturday. There'll be no-one at the Government
on a Saturday.

ASSISTANT ONE

You're right. But can it wait till Monday?

*Brief dramatic but muted chord.*

DIRECTOR

If it's a genuine message and it's waited a thousand
years, it can wait another forty-eight hours.
And if it isn't a genuine message it doesn't really
matter anyway, does it.

ASSISTANT ONE

Er, I'm not sure they're the only alternatives,
Director. Sir, er.

ASSISTANT TWO

If you want a complete silence ban, sir,
can we at least have that radio off.
*Right now.*

31. INT. BRIAN'S HOUSE. KITCHEN.
WRITTEN:

*Final chord is cut off as Dramatic Music abruptly stops.*

RADIO 3 ANNOUNCER VOICE:
*(just a trace of cultured weariness)*
That, I'm afraid, is all we are able to broadcast of
Maurice Van's twelve-hour marathon composition,
left tragically unfinished after his unexplained
disappearance during extensive rehearsals a year
ago. His perhaps posthumous 'Fourth Harmonica
and Pneumatic Drill Concerto, If I had a Sledge-
Hammer', was played by the massed bands of the
Coldstream Guards and —

*Brian turns the radio off. Brian and Alex are sitting at the breakfast
table, which is littered with used cups and very burnt toast.
The cups are arranged in a basic neural net formation.*

BRIAN
*(finishing a long explanation and still moving cups around
like an old general re-playing battles:)* So, basically,
a neural net is a piece of hardware, a lot like a brain,
made up of connections that can be modified as the
hardware goes through a learning process. And the
really crucial thing is that, unlike normal computers,
there's no separate software or program, just a new
configuration of the hardware itself that produces
the required result. So it takes time to train a neural
net, like training a human baby to talk, and with a
really big neural net, one with anything approaching
the number of connections in a human brain, we
simply wouldn't know just how the net has really
reconfigured itself, any more than we really know
how the human brain works. Is this getting any
clearer?

*Three flashing buttons, red, white, and blue, briefly appear in corners of the screen. Alex swats them away like flies.*

> ALEX
> My brain hurts.

*Ring at doorbell.*

> ALEX
> Saved by the doorbell! At last. That'll be Chrissie.
> Are you sure all the security controls are off?
> She won't get electrocuted if I let her in?

> BRIAN
> Might be my visitor instead. He's due at eleven.
> I'll turn security off while you go and see.

## 32. INT. BRIAN'S ROOM.

*Brian goes to his room and on his security monitor he watches Alex let Chrissie into the hallway. Brian just manages to de-activate various deadly devices in time, attending to an array of switches and buttons with suitably lurid labels. Including : 'Home Alone Configuration'.*

*Alex enters Brian's room with Chrissie. She is now a brunette again. Stunning outfit. She looks around, impressed.*

> BRIAN
> Hello. Again? I'm Brian, Alex's father.

> CHRISSIE
> I'm very impressed. By the computers, I mean.
> I'm Chrissie. Again. Alex tells me you chase bugs,
> viruses, hackers. Is that what all this gear is for?

> BRIAN
> Partly. I also develop my own physical equipment.

Er, I mean, my own security hardware. Too many people rely on just firewalls and virus-checkers to protect their data. They forget to guard the actual equipment itself. I try to do both.

                    ALEX
This house is like an experimental electronic fortress, wall to wall protection, 24/7.

                    CHRISSIE
At least Erika would be safe here then!

                    BRIAN
Erika? Are there, er, two of you? Sort of, er. . .

                    ALEX
No, Dad. Her laptop is Erika.

                    BRIAN
Ah, Eureka.

*Doorbell rings again. Brian looks at a security monitors, which is showing huge eye-retinas.*

                    BRIAN
That'll be Cotter. Chrissie, I'm afraid I have a meeting right now. Alex will show you the room. Stay for lunch if you like.

                    ALEX
Are you quite sure lunch is a good idea, Dad?


33. EXT. BRIAN'S HOUSE.

WRITTEN:
                    10.59 A.M.
                    *changes to:* "11 O'CLOCK. PRECISELY."

*Precisely as it does so, Harry Cotter presses the doorbell again.*

*He is 30-ish, very British, nondescript, and very prim and proper, in a dark brown suit, brown shoes, brown tie, white shirt. Dark brown sunglasses. Carrying a dark brown attaché case. An accountant by nature. Meticulous, anal, and paranoid.*

*With him is an attractive 20-something very American Carol Lewis, also all in brown, but a very fetching version of trouser-suit-cum-combat-gear (Avengers Mrs Peel). She believes in Proper Procedure.*

*Brian opens the door. Looks at them. Weak joke:*

> BRIAN
> Mr and Mrs Brown, I presume.
> I'm Jason Brorne, sorry, Brian.

> COTTER *(unamused)*
> No, Brian. Cotter. Harold Cotter. This is Lewis,
> Carol Lewis. She's on the job with me.
> I'm sorry  we came a fraction early.

> BRIAN
> It happens. Er, not at all, do come in.

> CAROL
> Shouldn't you check our biometric IDs first?

> BRIAN
> Well, the door-cam has already read your rectal,
> er retinal images, and the door-bell has checked
> his fingerprints. So I can vouch for your really
> being who you think you are. Remember, I'm in
> security myself.

*He lets them in.*

34. INT. PLEASANT UPSTAIRS ROOM.
DOUBLE BED, WARDROBE, DESK.

*Alex is showing Chrissie the room.*

ALEX

Would this suit? There's a bathroom just along the
hall. No telephone or television points I'm afraid,
but there is a power socket for Erika.

CHRISSIE

Don't need a phone line. Erika's got her satellite
modem. Built into the umbrella. Her batteries last
a month or two. And I've got my mobile.
The room looks fine to me. What about cooking?

ALEX

That's a very interesting question.

35. INT. BRIAN'S ROOM.

COTTER

There have been some major developments
overnight, Winston. We need absolute secrecy
for what I am about to show you. Sir Gerald assures
me this house is electronically secure. Is that so?

BRIAN

Absolutely. I already had a phone call from Sir
Gee-gee this morning. Told me about the NATO
exercise cock-up last night. Anything new since?

LEWIS *(scandalised)*

A phone call from Sir Graham-Gregory?
On an open line? That's pretty irregular.

BRIAN

Don't worry. All my outside communications
are automatically scrambled. I work from home,
after all. And security *is* my business.

COTTER

Well, you won't have seen the latest data
from HETI. It's quite disturbing.

*Cotter opens a very basic laptop and begins incompetently to show a poor Powerpoint presentation of screen shots of some of the HETI data from previous scenes.*

## 36. INT. FRANK'S ROOM.

*Loud rock music. Frank is at various computers simultaneously. On one monitor is the H.E.T.I. website, showing only a 'Temporarily Unavailable' message. Close-up of another monitor : cross-fade to a live webcast, which fills the whole viewing screen, from:*

## 37. FULL ON-SCREEN:
## INT. SOFTWARE CONVENTION. [EARLS COURT]

## WRITTEN ON WEBCAST:

CORPORATE CONSUMER
COMPUTER CONVENTION

*Time-counter in corner of screen shows [e.g.] 11.07 a.m.
[This changes in real time so that 11.11 occurs at "XX" below]*

*Screen format is in the style of 'Youff' interactive TV lay-out. Multiple irritating scrolling and animated text-boxes all superimposed on the webcast indicate that the speaker is:*

*TOM BANE, American 36 year old multi-billionaire CEO of SoftCorp Inc, giving the launch address for SoftCorp's new flagship product.*

*Main part of the screen shows a live video feed from the convention:*

*Suitable graphics come up on a huge screen behind Bane while our viewing screen (as Frank's monitor) continues to show endless additional information, using every trendy appalling web-design device.*

*Frank's super-imposed mouse-pointer zaps pop-ups as they appear, etc.*

BANE  (*in mid-cliché-ridden-speech:*)
. . so the future of global corporate computing
lies with the radically innovative new forms of
image-processing applications, and above all
with our major new development launched today.

At last, Softcorp, in association with our new
partners, MonoCorp, brings you the internet search
engine you didn't even know you've been searching
for. "Patriarch".

Patriarch allows you to match any image datum,
to search on visual matching, to find the precise
patterns of image information that you want.
That includes pictures, diagrams, any patterns of
visualisable dataflow.

*Suitable accompanying images illustrate and stridently advertise the*
*following:*

> You want to check out a potential employee.
> Feed a photo offen your security camera and
> *prestissimo*, Patriarch will match it with the new
> SoftCorp Global ID Service, linked to every
> employment and law-enforcement ID bank globally.
>
> Want to locate that elusive clip-shot just right for
> your marketing operation?  Feed Patriarch with a
> rough sketch and it will find the so-so-beautiful
> counterpart your own team couldn't design or
> dream up. SoftCorp offers a copyrighted Global
> Image Databank of the best 100 million digital
> images and video-clips ever devised.
>
> You want to check out the shape of a stockmarket
> situation, compare it with the historically available
> data. Done in seconds. And our partner MonoCorp
> will provide the Wall Street Visual Dataflow
> Database for you to search on.

And with SoftCorp's new Leisure Services On-line Dater-Partner, if you want to find that elusive woman of your dreams—or man—just feed in a rough verbal description: For example, "The most desirable bachelor on the planet": and Eureka!

*A huge smirking picture of himself comes up on the huge screen behind him. [ the "XX" mark: Time-counter ticks to: 11.11.]*

And the right answer! Found in just two micro-seconds across the globe.

But, seriously, folks. You could use Patriarch to search not just for new friends, but for lost loved ones, missing persons or pets, escaped criminals, even track down those sad elusive celebrities trying to travel *incognitissimo*.

*Appropriate clips from* Notting Hill *(e.g.) appear in supplementary screen-boxes. The vast image of Bane stays on the screen behind him.*

And our partner MonoCorp will soon offer the facility to do on-line real-time searches, with access to all the surveillance camera networks throughout every major city on the planet.

And we're proud to say that your very own London City has already run a successful pilot for that service. In close cooperation with your wonderful Metro Police and, of course, with every respect for the innocent British citizen's civil liberties. And from tomorrow MonoCorp will be launching similar services covering New York, LA, Tokyo, Paris, Berlin, Hartlepool, and soon the entire planet will be wired for: Patriarch!

OK, now I'll take just three questions from the press here, and one from on-line.

PRESS ONE
Why is it called Patriarch, Tom?

BANE
No great reason. We just ran out of catchy names,
and that one hadn't been used so far. I like it.
Good ring to it, don't you think.

PRESS TWO
What's the technical basis of this search engine,
Mr Bane? How can you possibly search on such
huge amounts of visual data so quickly?

BANE
Well, I ain't giving away trade secrets!
All visual query data is fed through to
SoftCorp's own massive servers and they do
the search-and-match for you.

PRESS THREE
So you mean, sir, the program isn't available
except through SoftCorp on-line? So SoftCorp
gets to file all the data sent to your service?
And you're not offering a version for local use
on my own machine and on my own data?

BANE
No, 'cos there ain't no such program.
In fact there ain't a program at all.
The SoftCorp servers are all neural net machines.
It's their internal configuration that allows the
search and match. You cain't transfer that to low-
end machines at all. But we do of course guarantee
—you have my personal word for it—that we will
respect all appropriate commercial confidentiality
in our operations. And now an on-line question.
Let's see. A Mr. fd1 has got in first, I think.

ON-LINE VOICE of Frank:
Frank Dickson. A non-technical question, Mr Bane.
When did you have the eye transplant?

BANE
I'm sorry. I don't follow.

FRANK
Look at the screen behind you.
Your eyes are greeny-grey up there. Not blue.

BANE
(*looks, is startled, but makes a quick recovery:*)
Well, I admit nobody's perfect. I just prefer greeny-grey. Digitally speaking. (*laughs it off but is puzzled*)
OK, no more questions. You can all try out
Patriarch for yourselves on the on-line search
machines installed around the convention,
compliments of SoftCorp.

38. INT. FRANK'S ROOM.

*Pull back from Frank's monitor. Frank is looking thoughtful, and appalled. Frank phones Alex.*

39. INT. ALEX's ROOM.

*Alex's mobile phone rings. Alex answers it. It is Frank..*

*[The following sequence begins as an old-fashioned cinematic split-screen with // indicating co-locations, but it gradually gets more and more complicated, and eventually out of hand.*

*Moving red borders around screen-boxes indicate which image has the soundtrack—as in old BBC multi-screen format.*

*If preferred, the sequence moves into multi-image digital flying or rotating or spinning image-cubes etc. etc. ]*

40.    FRANK ROOM // ALEX ROOM

//INT. FRANK:
>                    FRANK *(on phone)*
> Have you been watching the Bane webcast?
> They've finally launched Patriarch. But it's a lot
> more than a search engine. It's a data dictatorship.
> Pretty terrifying.

// INT ALEX:
>                    ALEX *(on mobile phone)*
> I can't log on. I'm grounded. No modem.

//INT. FRANK:
>                    FRANK
> This is important. Use plan B

//INT ALEX:
>                    CHRISSIE (in Alex's room)
> Plan B?

>                    ALEX (rapid)
> Something Frank cooked up for me.
> My dad may be a security expert but he doesn't
> realise he has an internal mole. When he thinks
> I'm grounded I can actually rig up a back-door
> network connection between my machine
> and one of Dad's. Frank told me how.

*Alex begins to set up the arrangement:*

> My computer shows up as one of my Dad's
> on his local network. So long as he's not actually
> using that machine I can then piggy-back onto
> his net access and he doesn't even realise.

41. NOW TRIPLE SPLIT SCREEN [Frank/Alex/Brian
rooms] AND GETTING CROWDED.

/// INT. ALEX'S ROOM:

*Alex sets up arrangement, Frank directs him as necessary over the phone. Rapid techno-gobbledygook exchanges about LAN configurations and WEP passphrases etc.*

///INT. BRIAN'S ROOM:
WRITTEN: 11.16.01 a.m. *(e.g.)*
[*this time changes in real time during the following sequence*]

> COTTER
> These separate incidents are far too scattered to be the work of a single maverick hacker.

> BRIAN
> So it's more likely to be a virus or a bug, yes.

> COTTER
> I *meant* that it must be a *whole global organisation.* Look, we're supposed to leave you the new data from HETI and NATO. But first I insist that you isolate your computer from all means of outside communication. It's far too risky to rely on scrambling. And no wireless links either.

> BRIAN
> That's paranoid. But if you really insist.

///INT. ALEX'S ROOM.

*Alex has just finished setting up the LAN link .*

42. ////*Now hopelessly multiple split screen showing changing combinations of: Alex's Room / Alex's Monitor / Brian's Room / Monitor Of One Of Brian's Machines / Frank's Room / Etc.*

*This sequence should be like a very fast and slick Brian Rix Whitehall farce. Written times in corner(s) of screens give exact second-by-second real-timings. Throughout, cheerfully upbeat music.*

////INT BRIAN'S ROOM . WRITTEN: 11.16.03 (e.g.)

*Brian links Cotter's laptop to his networked machines.*

> BRIAN
> OK, you can transfer the new data to the machine
> over there. It's Cheetah on the network.
> I'll disconnect the phones, ISDN, cable,
> wif-fi and the rest. Satisfied?

*Brian unplugs phone lines, etc., just as :*

////INT. ALEX'S ROOM . WRITTEN: 11.16.06 (e.g.)

*Alex's machine's screen becomes Cheetah's screen as Alex tries to get
onto the internet via the link to Brian's machine.
But overall internet connection has just been pulled.*

////INT. BRIAN'S ROOM. WRITTEN: 11.16.09 (e.g.)

*Harry copies data to Cheetah machine.*

*We see on the various screens that it is actually copying to Alex's
machine. The usual dramatic copying bar, but linking across two of the
split screens.*

////INT. ALEX'S ROOM. WRITTEN: 11.16.15 (e.g.)

*Alex sees new HETI data as it is copied over by Harry.*

> ALEX
> Wooops.

////INT. TRAIN CARRIAGE.

*Suddenly screen of the interior of a train replaces the split-screen from
Frank's room.*

*A total stranger is making a phone call on a mobile video-phone.*

>           TOTAL STRANGER *(to audience)*
>           Do you mind! I'm on the train!

*That part of screen reverts to Frank's room.*
*Frank is surprised and tries to work out what just happened.*

////INT. ALEX'S ROOM. WRITTEN: 11.16.18 (e.g.)

*Alex disconnects the LAN link. The Cheetah screen goes blank,*
*then reactivates as Cheetah, not as Alex's machine.*

*End of manic split-screen sequence.*
*Revert to gradually slower cutting between separate locations.*
*Music tempo slows.*

43. INT. BRIAN'S ROOM . WRITTEN: 11.16.19 (e.g.)

>           COTTER
>           Right, I'll leave you with it. You only have till
>           this afternoon for a preliminary analysis.
>           We're to report to a meeting of the
>           Alien Reports & Surveillance Evaluation committee.

>           BRIAN
>           A.R.S.E.?  Yes, GeeGee told me. At Lord Anglia's
>           place, 3 o'clock. I can give you both a lift
>           if you like. We can compare notes on the way.

>           COTTER
>           Fine. Pick us up, 2.15 at the regional office.

*Cotter and Carol leave.*

44. INT. ALEX'S ROOM.

>           ALEX *(to Chrissie)*
>           Never use Plan B. Always stick to Plan A.

## 45. INT. BRIAN'S ROOM

> BRIAN
> OK, let's see what we've got.

*Tries to find the data that has just been copied over. Can't.*

> Where the hell did he put it?
> Should be on Cheetah's S-drive.

*Baffled. He leaves the room to call Harry back.*

## 46. INT. ALEX'S ROOM.

*From his window, Alex sees his father leave to catch Harry,*
*But Harry is already driving off. Alex quickly re-establishes the link*
*to the Cheetah machine and copies the HETI data back over just*
*before Brian returns. But he also keeps a copy on his own machine.*
*[Briefly revert to the split screen to show the copying bar across.]*

## 47. INT. BRIAN'S ROOM.

*Brian comes back into room. Goes to Cheetah.*
*This time easily accesses HETI data. Even more baffled. To self:*

> BRIAN
> I must be going barmy. Or someone's playing
> games. Pretty clever games, too. How can they have
> hacked into my systems? I'm not even on-line.
> *(pause)* I need a good strong coffee. And lunch.

## 48. INT. ALEX'S ROOM.

> CHRISSIE
> Was all that really necessary, Alex?
> If you wanted to get onto the net,
> you could have just used Erika, you know.
> She's got a permanent satellite connection.

ALEX

Now she tells me.

*She fires up her laptop and quickly makes a connection to the end of the webcast from Earls Court convention. Cross-fade to:*

49. INT. SOFTWARE CONVENTION.

*Bane is trying to pacify a vociferous press corp who have been getting odd results from their Patriarch searches.*

BANE *(getting exasperated)*

No, there really are no bugs in the system.
There *can't* be bugs in this kind of system.
The prototypes have been running for nearly a year.
And there's no programs to hack into.
How can I explain it if everyone on the net
has suddenly got greeny-grey eyes—

50. INT. ALEX'S ROOM.

CHRISSIE *(logs off, angrily)*

Egotestical bastard.

ALEX

Who? Bane? What's gotten into you, then?

BRIAN'S VOICE *(calling from below)*

Alex, can you get some lunch together. Pronto.
I've got a meeting to get to this afternoon.
Ask Chrissie, if she wants to stay.

51. INT. BRIAN'S ROOM.

BRIAN *(to himself, puzzled)*

Odd the way things seem to happen around 10
or 11 in the morning. Well, if that's the pattern,
at least there won't be anything else happening
before this afternoon's meeting.

## 52. EXT. DEEP BENEATH THE ATLANTIC.

*A huge submarine is creeping silently through murky deep waters.*

WRITTEN:

> MOBILE HEADQUARTERS,
> DEFENCE MISSILE SHIELD COMMAND.
> USS SUBMARINE SHIELD,
> SOMEWHERE BENEATH THE ATLANTIC.
>
> TIME: 10.01
> (ADJUSTED EASTERN MILITARY STANDARD TIME)

## 53. INT. SUBMARINE.

*The Command room with scores of computers and gadgets.*
*But only two humans. Large screens show incoming 'missiles'*
*in ever-changing but by now familiar (Smiley) formations.*
*Explosions of light flashing all over the boards.*
*A miniature clone of the Wargames control room.*
*Sirens blare stridently.*

> COMMANDER *(white, Southern red-neck)*
> Godamn, damn, damn, and damn-it.
> Cross yor fingers. And say yor goddam prayers, boy.
> Might be yor last time.

> DEPUTY *(black, calm, cool, smart)*
> Should we not tell the President, sir?

> COMMANDER
> Why? He cain't do nuthing withouten our say-so.

> DEPUTY *(quiet sarcasm)*
> How about the British Prime Minister, then?

> COMMANDER
> You *must* be joking. Ways too late anyways.
> Counter-missiles already on their sweet ways.
> Whole system's gone automatic. Ballistic.

DEPUTY
So whatever happened, sir, to BIFSORDM?
The built-in fail-safe over-ride delay-mechanism?

COMMANDER
Damn time of the month. Y'know. DMS.
Darn Maintenance Schedule. It's being repaired.
How was I to know?

DEPUTY
More missiles incoming, sir. We're looking into
the jaws of the abyss here, sir.

*They watch the big screen. The missile dots keep coming.*
*The explosions of impact get more elaborate and rapid.*

*WRITTEN across bottom of screen, loop-scrolling:*

*...Please do NOT press ANY Red Button at this time...*

COMMANDER
Hell is sure a-popping! Our counter-counter-
missiles just pass straight through 'em.
There goes another batch! Geepers!! — We just
goddam got one, boy!! See, that explosion, there!

DEPUTY
Sorry, sir, but that was one of our own satellites, sir.
More incoming, sir. Lots of them on the big board.
What do you think we should do now, sir?

COMMANDER
Get it goddam over with, I suppose. *(he reaches for a*
*big red button, then pauses. Resignedly :)* Shit.

DEPUTY
No shit, sir. That red button won't do anything any
more, sir. We're completely out of the loop.
The system will just keep firing till it runs out of

all its anti-anti-anti-missiles. And we're down to our
last Firelighter already, sir.

COMMANDER
That's two hundred billion dollars worth of missiles,
boy. This'd better not be a false alarm.

DEPUTY
It better had be, you mean, sir.

*A bust of absolute light obliterates the big screen
and the cinema screen fades rapidly to black.*


54. INT. KITCHEN IN BRIAN'S HOUSE

WRITTEN:
STILL HERE.
LUNCHTIME.
AN ILLUSION.


*A High Noon kitchen clock shows 12 noon.
Radio in background is playing music of 'My Darling Clementine'.*

*Some fairly stale bread and very old cheese on the table.
While they try to eat it:*

BRIAN
Bit of a scratch lunch isn't it, Alex?
Couldn't you at least have toasted the cheese?

ALEX
*(is vigorously dosing cheese with ketchup, brown sauce, salad
cream, and mustard.)* No need. *(to Chrissie)*
Told you lunch would be a bad idea.
Neither of us can cook and we both hate shopping.

CHRISSIE
I can cook.

BRIAN (*enthusiastically*)
Do you want the room? You can have it rent-free
if you do some of the cooking.

CHRISSIE
Better than a discount at the Momtaz.
OK, I want the room.

ALEX
You're on probation: you can cook dinner tonight!

BRIAN
Move in when you like.

CHRISSIE
Well, it won't take me long to pack.
Coupla suitcases. At the Momtaz.

BRIAN
That's fine. I can pick your stuff up after lunch.
On the way to my meeting. I'll bring it back here
after the meeting. OK?

ALEX
Dad, can you drop us off at Kettles Yard?
I promised to show Chrissie my favourite spot
in Cambridge. And the best cure for a hangover.

BRIAN
And how would you know?

ALEX
That's what *you* called it.

55. EXT. STREETS.

*Rapid sequence: outside the Momtaz, Brian puts Chrissie's two
battered suitcases into the boot of his car.
Then drives to near Kettles Yard and drops Alex and Chrissie.
Then drives off to pick up Cotter and Lewis.*

56. INT. KETTLES YARD.

> ALEX
> (*showing various works to Chrissie :*)
> Kettle's Yard has all the best paintings in
> Cambridge, at least since the Kings' College Rubens
> was stolen. Used to belong to a guy called Jim Ede,
> who knew all these artists in Paris. Before they
> became big names. He'd buy stuff for the price of
> the canvas, or they'd just give him stuff they
> couldn't sell. Worth millions now. For years he
> simply opened up his house to anyone who just
> rang the door-bell. Now it's owned by the university
> but it still feels like coming into someone's home.
> My dad helped on the security systems for it.
> I just love to come here.

57. EXT. OUTSIDE COTTER'S OFFICE.

*Brian picks up Cotter and Lewis. Cotter goes to the boot to put
their briefcases and laptops away. As he opens the boot,
one of Chrissie's suitcases springs open, showing female lingerie.
Cotter is most perturbed. Sniffs at the strong smell of perfume.
Gets into the car and gives Brian a very cautious look.*

58. INT. KETTLES YARD.

> ALEX
> It's great to see real art, not digital reproductions.
> And it's still free. Since SoftCorp bought all the
> reproduction rights to most decent pictures in the
> world, they won't publish any actual art books.
> And I'm fed up having to pay to look at them on
> the SoftCorp website, with that bloody great
> SoftCorp logo plastered all over them as well.
> At least these haven't been bought up, yet, by
> SoftCorp. Keep Kettle's Yard Free!

CHRISSIE
Remind me to show you that art program
I mentioned.  Would anybody mind if I did
a bit of digital reproduction myself?

*Erika, even in furled umbrella mode, has a powerful built-in
digital camera. Chrissie starts taking lots of pix into Erika.*

## 59. EXT. CAR DRIVING. COUNTRYSIDE.

*Brian is driving Cotter and Lewis to Lord Anglia's home
at Filtchlings, deep in the Norfolk countryside.*

LEWIS
So why is ARSE meeting at Lord Anglia's place?
Who is this Lord Anglia anyway?

BRIAN
You'd know him better as Oliver Burton,
the film actor. Remember he made millions for a
walk-on bit-part in *Alien Gore: An Incredible Truth*.
He's a bit senile these days. Gets confused.
Thinks he was actually abducted by aliens.
Not just in the film.

LEWIS
But what's he got to do with the Alien Surveillance
Committee?

BRIAN
He gave huge donations to both Labour and Tory
parties. Told you he was confused. So they jointly
rewarded him with the 'important job' of chairing
a totally toothless 'UFO Investigation Committee'.
But now he's actually called a meeting, and Sir
GeeGee's going along with it. Any rate here's
Filtchlings, his little place in the country.

*Pull back to reveal arrival at a huge estate, with an enormous long
drive leading to a classic stately home and a moated castle.*

## 60. EXT. FILTCHLINGS

*The sequence at Filtchlings involves as many film-related elements and allusions as you can imagine, for example :*

*Visible in the gardens are an Edward Scissorhands look-alike, complete with shears, clipping hedges; and a Lawnmower Man going berserk on a motorised lawnmower, mowing crop circles into the lawn and yelling "Contact!".*

*101 dalmatians are running around. Pursued by 3 deer hunters. A Civil War enactment troupe are battling away. Japanese actors in Tudor costumes are doing the balcony scene from Romeo & Juliet. A David Sharkey is doing a piece to camera. Whatever. Camera crews are scattered across the grounds.*

*On the lawn in front of the house is a long table with a spotless white tablecloth, laid for a very French lunch. A Chabrol scene. Bunuel-like semi-naked women at the lunch table, seated on portable w.c.'s. Surrounded by an exasperated film crew trying to get a massive lighting rig to give the impression of a sunny French setting. Hopeless.*

*For the rest of this scene, one Camera becomes obsessively focussed on these women, constantly turning away from the shot to zoom onto them and being yanked back.*

*Meanwhile menacing-looking black helicopters [obviously CGI] are whirring overhead and dropping off delegates to the meeting, Apocalypse Now style, to the sound of Wagner on speakers, blasting the attempted idyllic peace of the Chabrol scene.*

*LORD ANGLIA, a very upright look-alike of any star actor (Olivier e.g.), meets Brian, Lewis and Cotter on the steps of the house.*

*He has two smoking antique shotguns under his arms. Hands these to SAM the Butler. Vaguely waves at the chaos all around. Clipped aristocratic tones.*

ANGLIA
Terribly sorry for the mayhem. Got to make ends
meet, y'know. Better than having bloody tourists
all over the place. (*gestures at the Chabrol table scene*)
Doing a dog food advert. Or laxative. Or cancer.
Busy weekend. That lot (*helicopters*) making a film.
I think. Got bookings for four weddings and a bar-
mitzvah this afternoon.

LEWIS  (*shouting over noise of helicopters*)
Carol Lewis, your Honour. Lovely place.
How do you get the lawn so neat and tidy?

ANGLIA
No problem, m'dear. Constant gardening.
Turn over the sod. Flatten it. Sow grass.
Bit of water. Mow it for four hundred years
—or so. Comes up a treat.

COTTER
Four hundred years. I see. And how long has it
been in your family, your Grace?

ANGLIA
Not long really. Only since my wife's third husband
won it. A golf bet, I believe. Let me show you in.

61. INT. FILTCHLINGS.

*Lord Anglia ushers them across the enormous hall to very high large
double doors, and opens them. Blast of full orchestra and very loud
massed choirs, singing Handel's Messiah.*

*The Butler, Sam, intervenes, (look-alike for either Sam Fuller or
Anthony Hopkins, as the butler in Remains of the Day):*

SAM
I'm most sorry, m'lud, but the London
Philharmonic is recording in the Regency Room.
And the Parlour has the Moscow State Circus this

afternoon. So I've had to put the UFO committee into the small drawing room. The other delegates are already waiting, m'lud. *(opens doors into:)*

62. INT. ENORMOUS ROOM.
*(Banqueting House, Whitehall ?)*

*Huge antique tables are arranged in a semi-circle with Lord Anglia's throne-like Regency chair in the centre position, all facing a huge painting (the stolen Rubens, from King's College) on one wall. About ten international delegates seated round tables, with name plates.*

*Pan slowly along faces and name-plates during opening speech.*
*Same actor appears at beginning and end of line*
*Delegates are all blatant look-alikes:*
*[Casting has had fun with whatever cheap look-alikes are available. For example: -]*

*Mgr Paolo Banco, Vatican [= Peter Sellers, Heavens Above]*

*Lambet Walker, Swiss [= John Cleese]*

*Commander Bondage, Corsica [=Jane Bond, in bondage gear]*

*Brute Shaft, CIA [= bowler-hatted OddJob]*

*Matt Rix, Enterprises Virtuels [in Matrix gear]*

*Rogero Cormano, Min.Informatio [= Peter Cushing]*

*Hitch Cock, Private Investigator, Plucky Belgium*

*Andrei Rublev O'Sonavavitch, Chelsea F.C.*

*Dead Bored Guy, Society du Spectacle, Inc.*

*etc.*

*Sir GeeGee also present. Lewis, Cotter and Brian take seats.*

ANGLIA

Right, chaps. Like to welcome you all.
Sorry to drag you into the country.
This country, too, some of you overseas chappies.
But Whitehall's closed on Saturdays. So lent them
my place. Available for hire. Reasonable rates, what.
Any takers? Free next Wednesday. No?
Well, telephone any evening before *seven, Sam or I*
*(audible groan from delegates)* can take bookings.

*Sir GeeGee coughs discreetly. Anglia takes the hint. Delegates are*
*mainly trying to make their translation headphones work. They don't.*

ANGLIA *contiues:*

Sorry the simultaneous translation wallahs
haven't arrived yet. Probably lost somewhere.
So I'll speak slowly and loudly. That should do the
trick. Now, several theories buzzing round.
Got some meself, actually. Toy-boy story really.

*Sir GeeGee catches his eye.*

Maybe later. First, call upon two Brit experts
to give us benefit, whatnot. Need to show
any visuals, chaps? Just tell Sam, my Butler
wallah.

*He presses a button and the Rubens slides aside to reveal a huge wall*
*monitor. Currently live TV showing the racing from Newmarket.*
*Lord Anglia starts enjoying the race.*

Jolly good. Day at the races. *Pretty Boy*
should win this one, 4 to 1. I know the stable lad.
Pretty well, actually.

*Remembers the meeting. Presses a red button and the TV turns into a*
*huge computer screen.*

Sorry. Brian Winston first. No relation.

BRIAN

OK, let's begin with a look at the Friday morning
incident to highlight the problem.

*On-the screen a large map of East Anglia. Points to locations:*

Two F16s were scrambled to intercept an
unidentified something. From *here*. According to
their on-board navigation systems, they should have
been over Mildenhall and Lakenheath. *Here.*
But they were actually over Cambridge. Very
low over Cambridge. However, the real
problem wasn't there. It was here—
*(points to the Suffolk coast).* They crossed the
coastline from *USS Yangste Incident* at 10.01
but *this* is what the coastline looked like on
their navigational guidance systems:

*On-screen a large visual of how the coastline on the digital maps
in the pilots' navigation equipment was distorted, so that planes
went off-course by miles. The re-drawn coastline combines
'Smiley' & 'Profile' distortions, though not clearly so yet.*

Which is also, I suggest, what happened when,
Friday midnight, the NATO invasion exercise
also went so badly wrong.

*The visuals show a variation of the same distortion of the coastline.*

Their navigational systems were also showing the
Suffolk-Essex coastline *here*, when the actual coast
was *here*. That's pretty definite evidence of a fault in
the navigational software, but it may be intermittent,
so very difficult to detect. But we do have one clue:
the timing of these two incidents. 10.01 and 00.01
are both binary numbers. That may be significant.
Though quite how is beyond me at the moment.

LEWIS
Let me just butt in here, on behalf of the USA Gov.
This is not just a petty parochial problem of
Suf-folks and the United Kingdoms, ya know.
This involves Big Uncle Sam too.

ANGLIA
Sam? My Butler? —Sorry, carry on, Cleo.

LEWIS
You already know about the unfortunate,
shall we say, premature ejaculation of our missile
defence system this morning. Well, add two other
curious incidents in the night. An American,
an Am-er-ican I say, long-range bomber,
flying peacefully over Lake Superior, ditched in the
lake, having followed *this* outline of the lake,
instead of the real one.

*Brings up image on screen, before and after: of Lake Superior distorted
to look like an elongated face.*

At first, of course, we blamed Canada, but now
we're not so sure. And in the Japanese Inland Sea:
one of the Pentagon's peaceful fishing boats, despite
a *very* sophisticated guidance system, ended up here:

*Image of a large gunship in a shopping mall car-park; a sign saying
'Jurassic Parking Only'.*

— fishing in the High Street of a small Japanese
town which I am not allowed to name, even if I
could pronounce it. Its instruments showed *this* as
the shape of the harbour it was aiming at, instead of
*this*.

*Screen shows before and after modified coastline and harbour shape:
examples of 'profile' distortions, so that outline faces seem to have been
superimposed on the original map.*

Now, obviously, the US Gov cannot accept that
these incidents are due in any way to any faults on
our part. But since nobody, I mean no-body, on this
planet messes with Uncle Sam, there simply *must* be
an *extra-terrestrial force* at work—

COTTER *(interrupts as the voice of reason..)*
Now calm down, dear, that's way too far-out for
any sensible *British* explanation. But those last two
incidents do rather undermine Brian's hypothesis.
Obviously, we are *not* dealing with just a software
bug. The incidents are far too extended around the
globe for that. Neither the Atlantic anti-anti-missiles
nor the HETI events can be explained—except by a
*concerted and determined assault* by very well organised
and very sophisticated *global hackers. (goes strident:)*
Maligant hackers. Practising deliberate sabotage.
On our computers, our navigation systems,
our satellites, our airfields, our beaches, our wives,
our coasts, our back-yards, our—

ANGLIA *(excitedly cuts him off)*
I see what you mean, laddie. Can't have axes of evil
chopping away at our precious coastlines. Got an
award for Lowestoft. Agree with you. Matter of Life
and Death. Organised hackers, yes. Global, yes.
But these aren't the usual enemies, Ruskies, Irish,
loveable Liverpudlians. They're damned aliens!
These alien wallahs have all seen *Independence Day*,
y'know. Yes! They know how to implant a virus,
using little green buggies to attack us globally.
I know all about them, y'know. Some of you may
not be aware that I was myself the victim of an
outrageous abduction. *(Sir Geegee catches his eye.)*
Well, any rate, those blips at Stansted were a real
UFO contact. And Cambridge was the real target,
not a mistake. Cambridge, slap on the Greenwich
Meridian lay-lines. Centre of scientific talent.
More Nobel Prizes than the whole damned USofA
—well, in the good old days, of course. And it's

happened before, y'know. Am I the only one to remember the Mildenhall Incident of 1950? Er, '51, was it? And of course my own abduction. Did I ever tell any of you about that?

*Sir Geegee finally heads him off:*

SIR GEEGEE
*(in smooth-talking Alec Guiness committee-speak)*
I wonder if I might just say a word or two, my lord. Like you, I am moderately inclined towards the hacker sabotage hypothesis. And I might even add the mildly odd episode at the launch of Patriarch this morning, which doesn't quite fit the other patterns. But since I just happen to sit on several of the various boards of directors concerned, I can tell you, in strictest commercial confidence of course, that test versions of the Patriarch search engine have in fact been in use for some time by the organisations involved in these three main incidents. NATO, Air Traffic Control, HETI, and Monocorp itself of course, have all been using Patriarch in test mode. And this, I do think, somewhat tips the balance towards some sort of ghost in the machine. *(very smoothly manipulative:)* So, I would tentatively suggest that we might perhaps have a quiet word with my old friend Tom Bane about that possibility, before we go chasing after aliens, or even Liverpudlians. So I've taken the mild liberty of setting up a meeting, for tomorrow, at 11 a.m. If, say, Brian would care to represent us, perhaps he could report back to a re-convened sub-committee meeting, of, let's say, Lord Anglia and myself, at, shall we say, four o'clock tomorrow afternoon. I do hope that's in line with your own thinking, my lord.

ANGLIA *(miffed)*
Well, that all seems just a wee bit unilateral, I must say. Still think little green wallies involved, meself.

Maybe this Tom Bane is an alien entry-prenueur, like that chappie who fell to earth a few years ago. But, yes, OK, damnit, I'll go along with all that. So, summary of action, what? Brian to go and see this Bane fellah in London, see if his company somehow involved. Cotter here to pursue security breaches, hacking, etc. I'll think a bit more about alien buggeries meself.. Report back this time tomorrow. Fine. Any questions? Suggestions? Contributions? Alternatives? Do speak up!

*Other delegates try to get a word in, in various languages. (Sub-titles appear in multiple exotic languages and go haywire, jostling each other off the screen —)*

### ANGLIA
Sorry, can't understand a blinking word you're all saying. Need to get those translator chaps here on time tomorrow. *(remote activates live TV)* Meanwhile, the third race from Kempton Park should be on shortly. Do feel free to watch. Sam will take your bets. Actually, the winner will be *Buggerit*, 8 to 1.

## 63. INT. BRIAN'S HOUSE. LIVING ROOM

*Alex, Brian and Chrissie are watching the end of the early evening TV news, about 6.20 p.m.*

*The TV is showing a war report from Reg 'Mike' Dickson, apparently under heavy fire in some remote rough spot on the globe. Tough, seasoned war correspondent, grim-faced. Is ending his report:*

### TV: DIXON
As battle continues between these warring factions in this still bitter armed truce, this is Mike Dixon, reporting from another forgotten conflict.

*Throughout the following exchange, the TV News continues with items A, B, C:*

ALEX [to Chrissie]
That's Frank's dad. Told you he was always off
reporting from somewhere exotic. Twelfth time
this month he's reported that forgotten war.
Can't seem to leave it alone.

TV ITEM A: *footage of spectacular fireworks-type flashes*
*high in the sky over the Atlantic.*

TV: ANNOUNCER
The White House are denying reports that the
controversial star shield system was finally tested
today. Commenting on a spectacular display of
explosions seen over the Atlantic, a Pentagon
spokes-robot dismissed the idea that the USA
would, as he/she put it, "jerk off thousands of
missiles just to test the goddam system". He/she
suggested that what was witnessed was a burst of
Northern Lights, the Aurora Borealis, normally seen
only over the Arctic, but this time unusually visible
as far south as the Cape of Good Hope.

CHRISSIE
I don't watch the news normally.
Never seems to be anything new on it.

BRIAN
It's a kind of civic ritual, watching the same things
happening again and again. Disasters, famines, wars,
riots, murder. It's kind of comforting, in its own
way. You're never on TV yourself, so these things
never happen to you.

ALEX
Dad's almost a news junkie. On the dot: 6 o'clock
news. Then dinner. Then back to work. Barely see
him in the evenings.

TV ITEM B:

TV: ANNOUNCER

The SoftCorp Corporation has dismissed reports
that its newly launched Internet Search Service
Patriarch has run into trouble. After an
embarrassing glitch at the opening of the London
Computing Convention, the multi-billionaire
founder of SoftCorp, Tom Bane, said that such
systems always had minor teething problems.
Only this time, he joked, they were eye-matching
problems.

*VTR of Tom Bane speaking at the convention, but the tape runs very
fast indeed, and Bane's voice is just a high-pitched gabble while images
flash past.*

TV: ANNOUNCER

I do apologise. We seem to be having a minor
technical hitch ourselves.. And now, finally —

BRIAN

Talking of dinner…

CHRISSIE

Everything's under control. It's in the oven.
Timed for the end of the news, just as you asked.

TV ITEM C:

TV: ANNOUNCER

— Buckingham Palace was mildly embarrassed
today when it was pointed out that the picture of
Her Majesty the Queen on the Buckingham Palace
web-site seems to have been tampered with by
hackers, and that the Queen was apparently smiling
with the enigmatic smile of the Mona Lisa.
*(image of collaged royal face shown on screen.)*
A spokeswoman said that the image had been
quickly rectified and that the Queen was her usual
smiling self again. —

And now the weather in your area —

CHRISSIE
Right, dinner time. Come and get it. One minute.

*She bustles off.*

BRIAN
Let me just get the local weather for tomorrow.
I have a meeting in London.

*On the TV: the weather maps for East Anglia are hopelessly distorted
as the weather forecaster struggles valiantly on, trying to match her
gestures with the constantly shifting outlines of the coast, while several
towns keep changing their locations on the weather maps as well.*

BRIAN *(snaps TV off)*
I give up! That's all we needed!

64. INT. BRIAN'S HOUSE. DINING ROOM.

*Alex and Brian are looking gloomily at their cold plates, with
very burnt chips and under-cooked fish.*

BRIAN *(sotto voce to Alex)*
Mine's ice-cold, Alex. Not even de-frosted.

CHRISSIE *(Jamie Oliver petulant)*
Well, I'm very sorry. I mis-read the recipe. I haven't
gotten used to your cooker yet. I mis-timed it. OK.
In any case I only said I could cook. I didn't say I
could cook properly.

BRIAN
It's the same thing, isn't it?
Like being a cobbler.

*Chrissie clears away the plates and puts bread and cheese on the table.*

ALEX *(changing the subject)*
Dad, if you're driving up to London tomorrow
can I have a lift please? I want to go to Tate
Modern again. Do you want to come too, Chrissie?
There's some fabulous stuff there.
Leger's *Ballet Méchanique* film is my favourite.

CHRISSIE
Well, I'd promised to go up and see my sister
anyway. It was her birthday yesterday. Come and
meet her. She developed that program I mentioned.
And if you want decent cooking, Brian, you'll have
to meet her too. She's a terrific cook.

BRIAN
I'll happily give you both a lift. My meeting's at ten,
and I have to be back here for about four.
But I could meet you at the Tate for lunch
and then drive you back, if that suits.
OK? Now I've got work to do tonight

CHRISSIE
And I've got to unpack. *(looks at remnants of barely-
eaten meal)* Do I still get to rent the room? *(nods of
agreement)* And then I can show you Rem-Brand
["Rembrandt"] as well, Alex.

BRIAN
Ram Brand?

CHRISSIE
It's an art program I promised to show Alex.

*They disperse to their different rooms.*

65. INT. BRIAN'S ROOM. *[brief]*

*Awful avant-garde music. Brian at various computers, working on
HETI and other data, mainly looking at maps, comparing hard-copy
atlas book with various digital maps on screens, from various websites*

*and from the incident data. He is very puzzled. The digital map data is clearly but subtly modified in several ways.*

## 66. INT. ALEX'S ROOM.

*Chrissie enters with laptop-unbrella, unfolds it with a flourish. The umbrella plays a Handelian trumpet fan-fare.*

> CHRISSIE
> And here is —REM-BRAND!
> *(goes into very-fast-talking salesman mode : )*
> Rem-Brand is the latest MAGNIFICENT product from world-beating Aye Eye Technologies.
> A new eye upon the world of digital image-making and manipulation. Astonish your friends. Put fear into your enemies. Digital global warping has finally arrived. *(begins to demo the program as she speaks)*
>
> All you need is a digital camera, an out-of-copyright set of Old Masters, an original Leonardo or Picasso, and you are definitely in business. *Rem-Brand* will take the authentic output of any artist, analyse its characteristic features, its individual style, its unique signature, and will quickly re-produce for you an exact living original—to the very same identical specifications.
>
> You want a Picasso for your kitchen, a Matisse for your conservatory, a Duchamps for your winecellar? Let *Rem-Brand* take the strain, evade the pain, produce the stain on the canvas, the laser-printed digital canvas. You will not know the difference. Neither would they. Picasso would have signed it himself, Leonardo acknowledged his own lost masterpiece. And as every street-savvy artist on the block gets their very own copy of *Rem-Brand* see how the auction houses will wilt under the pressure, new masterpieces emerging every minute, a whole *oeuvre* re-discovered every time you switch on your very own image-machine.

ALEX
Yes, Chrissie. But does it work?

CHRISSIE
Of course it works. You've seen how morphing
works, all those images transformed into each other,
your headmaster's face into that of a pig, your boss's
countenance into a donkey's backside. All done by
subtle adjustments, gradual minute modifications.
Well, *Rem-Brand* takes a series of paintings and
transforms one into the other until it has found the
exact fractal formula which allows it to take just that
one small step further for mankind, and then
another, and another—until it has magically
manufactured the next full-scale transformation.
Constable painted a hundred landscapes,
*Rem-Brand* will paint his one hundred and first.
Turner painted forty two sunsets, let *Rem-Brand*
create the forty-third.

ALEX
Show me.

CHRISSIE
Certainly sir. Let us just add another Rembrandt
self-portrait to that long distinguished line.
(*as she speaks, the screen scrolls through digital images of all
Rembrandt's self-portraits and then performs the procedure
described:* )
*Presto*: a collection of genuine Rembrandt self-
portraits, more or less, from youth to age, from
cradle to coffin. Yet, through it all, the
unmistakeable face of Genius itself, the eyes, the
nose, the nostrils, the quizzical expression, the
lopsided ears, that faint smile upon the lips, the
same bone structure beneath the superficial
fattenings of maturity, the permanent wave in the
hair as it greys and whitens, leaving a faint echo
even in his final baldness—

—Add them all together, add a variation of tone and colour, a shadow here, a nice poignant light falling across the face, a fine new lace collar, a tired bag or two under those unforgettable eyes—*et voila!!* An authentic Rembrandt, circa 1678.

                    ALEX
He died in 1669.

                    CHRISSIE
Even better! A posthumous self-portrait. Brilliant! Worth even more on the auction floor. Remember that a painter's reputation increases after his death. Now any artist worth his salt can carry on painting from beyond the very grave. Still lives, epic battles, wallpaper designs, whatever sells.

                    ALEX
Still lives, you said?

                    CHRISSIE
There's just one small drawback, though.
This is the only copy of the program.
And I can't really give it to you. It's actually  the neural net built into this one machine, Erika herself.

                    ALEX
So  Erika *is* the neural net Rembrandt—?

                    CHRISSIE
Yup—Sort of. And we had to train Erika's net for a whole year before it could even do a proper Rembrandt. And then we couldn't find any way to duplicate her net onto another machine. We were working on that problem when we went more or less bankrupt. Which is why I've got this prototype machine. And why I think Tom Bane is an egotistical bastard, since you asked. I'll tell you that story tomorrow. Or you can get it from Debbie. Have fun!

*Chrissie leaves and Alex settles down to explore Rem-Brand.*

## 67. INT. CHRISSIE'S ROOM

*Chrissie is getting undressed and into her bathrobe to go and get a bath.*
*The Camera tries hard to catch her momentarily nude but fails.*
*So we suddenly see the effect of re-winding a videotape, then held on*
*pause, then stop-frame advance. Still fails to freeze-frame nudity.*
*Gives up and fast forwards to Chrissie leaving her room to go for her*
*bath along the corridor.*

## 68. INT. ALEX'S ROOM

*Alex responds to phone call from Frank:*

>            FRANK *(audible on phone)*
> Been trying to mail you. Are you still grounded?
> What happened to Plan B? I've been trying to find
> out what's been going on at HETI, but their whole
> site is down. And all sorts of weird things have been
> happening. You'll have to get on-line, boyo.

>            ALEX
> Slow down, Frank. No, I'm not on-line again yet.
> Still grounded. And Plan B was nearly a disaster.
> But hang on, you wanted HETI data.
> Just thought of something. *(he checks the data that*
> *Cotter copied over onto his computer. Sees the HETI files)*
> I may have something for you, Frank. My Dad's
> been looking at some of that HETI data too.
> *(remembers that Erika has a built-in satellite modem)*
> And I may even be able to send it to you after all.
> Let me check something. Call you back.

## 69. INT. THE CORRIDOR BETWEEN ALEX'S AND CHRISSIE'S ROOMS.

*Chrissie is just heading for the bathroom, half-draped in a bathrobe,*
*as Alex comes out of his room looking for her.*

ALEX

Chrissie, I wanted to—erm— *(embarrassed as he realises that she's half-naked, but already committed )* Sorry. Er, how do I link up my machine with Erika, so I can use Erika to send some stuff to Frank?

CHRISSIE *(gathers robe around her)*

Bad Guy! OK. I'll show you. Easer than explaining.

*They both go along to Alex's room. Hold shot on empty corridor. Longish pause. Then Brian shouts up from below.*

BRIAN

Making coffee. Anyone want some?

*No reply. Brian appears from the stairway. Looks along the corridor. Just as Chrissie comes out of Alex's room, still bathrobed.*

CHRISSIE

Hello Brian. Just showing Alex how to—

BRIAN

Yes?

ALEX

How to use her Erika, Dad.

BRIAN

That's a new one. *(pause)* Coffee anyone?

ALEX & CHRISSIE

No. No thanks.

BRIAN

OK. Then. Goodnight. Both. Er. Sleep well. *Au revoir, mes enfants.*

*Brian watches as they go to their rooms and close their doors.*

## 70. INT. FRANK'S ROOM.

*Frank receives HETI material and other incident data from Alex.
Dictates e-mail back.*

> FRANK *(dictates)*
> Email. To: Erika@Aye.Eye.com. Begin.
> 'Thanks for HETI. Arrived safe. Frank.' End. Send.

*Begins to doodle with HETI star material, rapidly trying out various
software processes on it, mainly plain old Photoshop techniques.*

## 71. INT. ALEX'S ROOM.

*Alex now has Erika on-line and is searching the National Gallery
database using Rem-Brand. Camera zooms in on faces of various
women portraits. Alex realises that they all have Chrissie's eyes.*

> ALEX *(aloud, to himself)*
> But they all have Chrissie's eyes! Greeny-grey!
> She ought to see this.

*He starts to get up to go and fetch her. As he half-leaves his door,
Chrissie emerges from the bathroom, wet and half-draped in bathrobe.
Alex thinks better of it.*

> Tomorrow.

*Camera tries to follow Chrissie back to her room.*

> Tomorrow, I said.

## 72. INT. FRANK'S ROOM.

*Frank is still doodling, playing with data from the HETI and the
Stansted incidents. Using a graphics tablet and stylus.*

*Then, decisively, he rapidly joins up the dots on the Stansted and
HETI data, like a child's drawing game, and gets clear face patterns.
Smiley shapes. Excited.*

Then he switches to the coastal map and other data and begins to trace a line round the modified East Anglia and other coastlines—and gets clear face profiles. More excited. Thinks.

Then goes to the Buckingham Palace website and downloads picture of Queen. Then to webcast of Bane speech and downloads picture of Bane.

He composites the lips from the modified Queen (Mona Lisa) and the eyes from modified Bane (Chrissie's eyes) with the positional (Smiley) dots of eyes/nose/mouth from the HETI star positions and the outlines from the coastal shapes—and gets a strangely odd full-face composite portrait—

> FRANK *(exhilarated)*
> At last, *that's* their message! An alien self-portrait!
> That's what they *look like*!!! Alex has to see this!
> *(pauses for a long think)*
> Wait a minute. This is a real scoop!
> I think I need my Daddy!!

*Starts to make a videophone call from one of his computers.*

*CU on Frank's monitor as the call is made through a webcam: On the screen Mike Dickson is in close-up using his mobile phone to reply. There are sounds of rapid gunfire near him.*

> MIKE
> Hello, Frank. Unexpected pleasure.
> But I thought I told you not to ring me at work.

## 73. EXT. APPARENT WAR ZONE
## FROM THE EARLIER TV ITEM.

*As Mike talks on his mobile phone, the film camera pulls back to reveal him lounging at the pool-side of an ex-pat shooting club, somewhere in the tropics, with a gin-and-tonic and a young lady. The audible gunfire is from a clay-shooting competition in the near background. All very relaxed. None of this is visible to Frank on the close-up image from Mike's mobile phone.*

74. INT. FRANK'S ROOM.

                    FRANK
     Hello Dad. Hope the war's going well.
     I think I've got a scoop for you. Interested?

                    MIKE  *(on monitor)*
     Always the professional, son.
     If you've got a scoop, I'll happily sell it to the
     highest. Shoot. *(gunfire audible)* Sorry.

FADE TO BLACK]

               OPTIONAL COMFORT BREAK
                  *(with wine and cheese)*

                         *

75. FULL SCREEN  INT/ EXT/ *(ambiguous)*

FADE UP FROM BLACK.

*Extreme close-up of what seem to be swirling galaxies deep in dark space, with Milky Way type spirals.*

*Then :*  WRITTEN AS TITLE: S.U.N.D.A.Y.
*Add sequential sub-titles  [The Sting style:]*

> FOUR RAIDS
> AND A FEW
> MORE MEALS

*Pull back slowly to reveal that the swirling galaxies are actually swirling coffee in a coffee cup, held by Lady Sybil Anglia, in:*

76. INT. FILTCHLINGS. BREAKFAST ROOM.
WRITTEN:
> A LATE BREAKFAST.

> LADY SYBIL
> *(a Sybil Thorndike look-alike)*
> *(finishes talking on a phone:)*
> Of course, my darlings. No problem. 'Byee!
> *(to Sam the Butler)*
> Fill it again Sam. *(pause)*
> Fuller, Sam. I like it hot.

*Sam does so. Then goes to Lord Anglia, at the other end of the very long breakfast table, and hands him a massive pile of Sunday papers.*

*Lord Anglia begins to skim through them. They all have screaming headlines and photos of HETI star formations.*
*And the composite portrait from Frank's Photoshop exercise.*

*Various headlines, all marked as EXCLUSIVE!:*

> *Sun:*  THE FACE OF GOD!
> *Mail:*  THEY'RE HERE!
> *Mirror:* THE STARS HAVE SPOKEN!

*Star:*   LUCEY IN THE SKY!
*S.Times:*   ALIENS ALLEGED FIRST CONTACT.
*Telegraph:*   Unusual Image Perhaps Found In Distant Star
Cluster.
*Observer:*   THE FACE THAT LUNCHED A
THOUSAND THEORIES.

ANGLIA *(apoplectic)*
Outrageous. Who leaked!?

SYBIL
Not me, dear. I haven't been this morning.

ANGLIA
Sam. Put telly on, lad.

*Sam switches on a huge TV disguised as a Georgian sideboard.*

TV: NEWS ANNOUNCER
*(over shots from HETI of spectacular star formations,
with various strange faces superimposed:)*
—The constantly changing star formations are
being claimed by some as the sign of a new age
dawning, and the mysteriously beautiful face some
claim to see in the stars has aroused expectations of
a new female messiah. There are numerous reports
of wise women being seen coming from the east.
These are unconfirmed. World leaders are reported
to be considering an urgent joint statement, to be
published as early as a week on Wednesday.
Meanwhile the England team are again in deep
trouble. After yesterday's ball-swallowing incident,
the Umpires struck back today.

ANGLIA *(snaps TV off)*
That's it. Let me call a spade a spade, Sam.
Somebody let the cat out. This is Dark Matter.
Treacherous Treason. Fourth Man stuff. Long leg
boundary business. Sam, get Cotter. Dial M.

*Sam brings the phone over, dialling as he does so.*

> ANGLIA *(into phone)*
> That you, Cotter? Lord Anglia. No, not Ford
> Anglia. 'Lord, Lord'. Good Lord. Right.
> You've seen the papers. *Sunday* papers. Sunday
> bloody Sunday! Well, look at them, damnit.
> *(impatient pause)* Yes. *(very impatient pause)* Yes.
> *(exasperated pause)* Exactly. It must have been
> someone at that meeting. Or some other meeting.
> Precisely. Get them, Cotter. And play dirty, Harry,
> if you have to. I want this stopped. Now.

## 77. INT. HARRY COTTER'S OFFICE

*Large room with lots of not very impressive gear. About a dozen staff,
all dressed in various shades of brown. All bustling about being 'busy',
but it's patently not clear just what they are actually being busy about.
Cotter is reading newspapers. Calls over AIDE.*

> COTTER
> We've got to find out who leaked this story.
> That could be difficult.

> AIDE
> It says: Frank Dickson. On the bye-line, sir.

> COTTER.
> Oh. So who's Frank Dickson? Now, we've got to
> find *him*. Fast.

> AIDE
> It says, sir, see, at the bottom of the article,
> that he's the son of the paper's war correspondent,
> Mike Dickson.

> COTTER
> The television person-person? Find him. Find them.
> Do a search. Use that new MonoCop thingie.

                    AIDE
MonoCorp you mean sir. The anti-anti-terrorist
database?

                    COTTER
Yes. Find out all we know about him.

                    AIDE
All *we* know, sir? That's a bit paradoxical isn't it, sir.
I mean, logically, if we already know it, we wouldn't
have to find it out and if—

                    COTTER
Just get on with it. Get Hacker onto it.

*Aide goes to a side door and opens it. Blast of heavy metal music.
Cotter screams: Shut it! Aide enters and shuts door behind him.
Name on door: Pat Hacker, Jnr.*

## 78. INT. HACKER'S DEN

*HACKER is about 13, classic nerd-freak, surrounded by computer
gear, no windows, etc. Laid back. Heavy Metal music blasting.
Coke cans, crisp packets litter the entire room.*

                    AIDE   *(his father)*
OK, look son. Pronto. Everything you can get on
Frank Dickson, son of Mike Dickson, aka Reginald
Dixon, of Sum-Times Papers Ink. Move it, son.
Earn your pocket money. *(likes the music)*
Cool band, Luke. A band apart.

                    HACKER
Shut that door. Behind you.
And don't call me Luke, Daddy-O.

## 79. INT. HARRY'S OFFICE.

*Results of SoftCorp search coming up on screen. Surveillance images of
Frank in his wheelchair at several disabled rights demonstrations.*

                    AIDE
Looks pretty dangerous to me. The Militant
Disability Front. Out to cripple the system.

                    COTTER
I want full surveillance, audio, visual, nasal, the lot.
If his wheelchair squeaks I want to know it. *Now*.
And get that Pat—ah, here he comes.

*Instantly, Hacker saunters into the office. Thumps down an enormous
pile of paper onto Cotter's desk.*

                    HACKER
First dump from Dickson's ISP, boss-man.
Latest emails on top.

                    COTTER
You got that illegally, didn't you. Hacked into his
private files. How many times have I told you.

                    HACKER
That's what you pay me for, b'wana.

                    COTTER
What's this? *(reads last e-mail)*
"To Erika at Aye Eye.dot.com. Thanks for Heti.
Arrived safely. Frank." OK. Find out who Hetty is.
And who Erika is. Legally. If you have to.

                    HACKER
*(takes control of Cotter's computer)*
Already done that, chummie. Website of Aye Eye.
Picture coming up. She's called Debbie on the
website but probably a pseudonym.

                    COTTER *(to Aide)*
Right. Feed that *(picture of Debbie)* into SoftCop. See
what we've got on her.

HACKER
Already done that, matey. Results coming through
—now.

*Cotter's screen (and viewing screen, for us) starts filling with image after image of (real) news-footage: demos, protests, political campaigns, in all of which Debbie is highlighted, as is Chrissie. (CGI manipulation).*

COTTER
Bingo! Suffering F-*bleeped* Crickets Almighty!

AIDE
I beg your pardon, sir. Suffragette Cricket?

COTTER
An American expression, heard it on a film,
or somewhere. *(amazed at results)* Just look at this.
She's been involved in every damnable incident
and heinous crime for the last five years.
*(as results keep coming)* Er, ten years. Blimey.
Fifteen years. Good God! Grosvenor Square, 1968.

AIDE
That's the General Strike, sir. 1926. And that's Mrs
Pankhurst there, sir. 1910. I think we've got a pretty
busy little activist here, sir. Young for her age, too.

COTTER
But this is impossible. Unless..

HACKER
Reckon she's One of Them, then, old cobber.

AIDE
She does bear a striking resemblance to that
'Is This The Face of God' picture, y'know.

COTTER

Bloody nonsense. Get back to reality.
I want immediate armed raids—on this character
Frank Dickson, on the Aye Eye offices, and on any
other addresses we have for these cyber-terrorists.

HACKER

The Momtaz Restaurant and Curry House, mate,
Cambridge.

COTTER

What?

HACKER

She has a shady sister. Student. That's her address.
Raid that too?

COTTER

Yes. Yes. Bloody student, might have known.
And find Lewis, Carol. Christmas!—it's about time
she did something useful. Her lot can put a spoke in
this Wheelchair Frank fiend. I'll take out the
Momtaz Curry what-not myself. And put Special
Branch onto the London end. Chop chop.

80. EXT. OUTSIDE AYE EYE OFFICES IN
BARBICAN.
*[e.g. old Mahoney Associates building, Bridgewater Square, Barbican]*

*Brian drops Alex and Chrissie off in narrow side street, near the AI
office. Difficult to manoeuvre a car, since mainly a pedestrianised area,
with car barriers across roads. An underground car park entrance.*

BRIAN

OK. I'll meet you at Tate Modern, one o'clock.
If you need to contact me, I'll be at the Russell
Hotel, Bloomsbury. Ask for Tom Bane. (*drives off*)

ALEX

'Ask for Tom Bane' ! He's meeting Tom Bane.

CHRISSIE
Lucky I didn't know. Come and meet Debbie.
Not sure she'll be pleased that your Dad's
a friend of Bane's.

ALEX
But he isn't.

81. EXT. OUTSIDE FRANK'S HOUSE.
WRITTEN TITLE (as in *The Sting*) :

*The Raid (I)*

*Carol Lewis, in fetching combat gear (Lara Croft), is in charge of a
crack American force in full jungle camouflage, poised for an assault at
the gateway. The name on gates is now: Holly / Wood. They are
listening to horrendous (soundtrack) screams from within the house.
Walkie-talkie conversation (despite being only two feet from each other):*

LEWIS *(horrified at the sounds)*
What kind of people are we dealing with! !
Exercise extreme caution.

OFFICER
My men won't hesitate, sir, er, madam.
Just give the order, sir-madam.

*Deployment orders crackle over radios as troops take up assault
positions round the house.*

82. INT. FRANK'S ROOM

*Frank is monitoring the assault force's radio exchanges
without realising it's his house that is about to be raided.*

FRANK
Wow. This is getting exciting.

## 83. EXT. GATEWAY.

*Just as the assault is about to begin, a local middle-aged policeman, an old Morse or Dixon of Dock Green look-alike, arrives on his bike, swings into the gateway, and then stops when he sees armed blacked-up troops. Pondersouly takes off his bicycle clips and locks up his bike, while chatting avuncularly:*

> P.C. MORSE
> Ah, the Fifth Cavalry. Are you lot here about the noise complaints, too? Seems a bit heavy-handed. She's normally pretty reasonable about it. Just forgets when it's Sunday, and other people want to sleep.

> LEWIS
> Get away, you flannelled fool. This is none of your business. *(to troops)* Right, go go go!

*Assault begins. Mayhem at will.*

## 84. INT. MAGDA'S ROOM

*Armed troops burst through the windows, yelling and shattering glass. Magda starts screaming, even louder than her screaming film-track. P.C. Morse has casually sauntered in with the troops.*

> P.C. MORSE *(to Lewis)*
> Now you've made it a whole lot worse, miss. There won't half be complaints now.
> *(to Magda)* Shush, shush, dear.

## 85. INT. FRANK'S ROOM.

*Armed troops burst through the door. Lewis in charge. Frank is surrounded by combat troops all pointing automatic weapons directly at him.*

> LEWIS
> Don't move! You can't escape.

FRANK *(completely unfazed)*
*(he moves the wheelchair slightly—it squeaks very loudly,
and Lewis winces.)* You're joking, of course.
*(he smiles sweetly at Carol, while manipulating his
webcam to pan slowly up her body:)*
Well, hello. I'm Frank. And you are—

*Lewis suddenly sees herself on the live webcast from Frank's webcam
and hears her own voice from the radio monitor.*

> LEWIS
> And get that lascivious camera off me. I'm not
> having this operation broadcast round the globe!

## 86. INT. HACKER'S DEN

*Hacker is watching the live webcast.*

> HACKER
> Oh yes you are. *(picks up his phone.)*
> That Sum-Times News Ink? Put me through
> to the Leaks Desk, Tip-Off Section. *(pause)*
> Hello, Leaks? ID 5476 here. Usual account number.
> Oh, hello Charlie. Yes it's me. Good one for you
> today. Got a pencil?

## 87. INT. FRANK'S ROOM

*Lewis is interrogating Frank and Magda,
who has recovered her calm.*

> LEWIS
> Now, I warn you. I want a straight answer.
> Untied tongues. Spilt beans. Who is Erika?

> MAGDA
> Was that her name? That nice Irish girl,
> Wild Oscar Fingal O'Brien?

LEWIS
Irish? I.R.A?

FRANK
Ah. A.I., actually. Erika's a computer. Neural net.
Highly advanced artificial intelligence.

MAGDA
Was she indeed? *Very* advanced!
What will they think of next.

FRANK
*Human* intelligence? Maybe.

88. INT. AYE EYE OFFICES.

*Chrissie's sister, Debbie, is an attractive 30-something. She has been
explaining the bitter story of her ex-boy-friend, Tom Bane, and his
nefarious dealings with Aye Eye.*

DEBBIE
So that bastard Bane turned out to be a right, well,
bastard after all. But since there was no actual
software involved, we hadn't been able to copyright
the program, and since he'd taken our actual
machine, Paula, we had no proof anyway.
So he walked away with five years work.
And now he's released this Patriarch search engine.
Obviously based on my stuff. I don't know how
he's modified it, but he must have solved the
problem of cloning the neural nets that I couldn't.
What a birthday present!

CHRISSIE
Now he's gone public, I think it's time you exposed
him, Debbie. Go and confront him. Alex's dad
seems to know him. We could go straight over to
the Russell Hotel and have it out with him.

## 89. INT. EXPENSIVE SUITE AT THE RUSSELL HOTEL

*Bane is finishing his very different version to Brian:*

> BANE
> So. We spent millions developing this set of
> applications. They all needed massive neural net
> machines. Which only major corporates can afford.
> So we tested the prototypes through organisations
> that already had massive parallel processing power.
> Weather forecasting, satellite navigation, space
> imaging, crime prevention, and, yes, the military.
> It was a good deal for them and a good deal for us.
> Then we finally developed a way of cloning the nets
> onto our own distributed servers. But—
> and this is the crucial bit—
> *(flashing multi-coloured buttons appear & vanish.)*
> —this problem we're having *can't* be a virus.
> A neural net can't be attacked by a virus, a bug,
> a trojan horse. I keep explaining: there's no
> software, no program, to infect.
> *( single flashing red button appears. Vanishes.)*
> And why has all this only started happening
> just now? We've had beta versions operating
> without a hitch for nearly a year, but we finally
> go commercial And then this hits us.
> Look, here's what's been happening to SoftCorp's
> own databases since the launch yesterday.
> We finally took them off-line this morning.
> All the faces have the same damn eyes.
> The same mouth. The same ears even—

*Brings up thousands of facial images onto the immense screen of his
immense 'portable' laptop.*

> BRIAN *(looks closely)*
> I know those eyes. Girl called Chrissie.

BANE

What! Chrissie? Hang on.  *(peers more closely)*
Debbie, you mean! That's it! Aye Eye! Dammit.
*(Yiddish:)* —Ai Yi Yi!

90. INT. AYE EYE OFFICES.

DEBBIE

OK. Let's go get him. Alex, hope you can ride a
scooter? We don't like cars in this office. But we do
have some scooters for around town. Come on.

91. EXT. UNDERGROUND GARAGE.

*Debbie, Chrissie and Alex astride three slick Italian scooters, one red,
one white, and one blue. With on-board hands-free mobile phones.
Alex's has lots of outboard mirrors (Quadrophenia). They sweep out of
the underground garage and disappear round the corner just as:*

92. EXT. RAID ON AYE EYE.
WRITTEN: [*Sting* title:]

The Raid (Two)

*Armed Special Branch and an (L.A.P.D!) armoured car arrive in the
vicinity, but are blocked by the various anti-car blockades and barriers,
so can't get very close without difficulty. As they try clumsily to
manoeuvre the armoured car into position, nobody realises that Alex,
Chrissie and Debbie have just swept past them on the three scooters.*

*Finally the armoured car is lined up opposite the door of AI offices.
Officer in charge looks at watch.*

WRITTEN: *[time changes from]* 10.59 *[to]* 11.00

*Officer gives command and the armoured car fires at Aye Eye doors.
Nothing happens.*

OFFICER

You're supposed to blow the bloody doors off!

93. EXT. RAID ON MOMTAZ.

WRITTEN: [*Sting* style:]

Raid The Third

*(time changes from)* 10.59 *(to :)* 11.00. Again.

*Cotter and SAS-type troops are in a side street round the corner from the Momtaz. Cotter checks his watch, and orders the SAS troops into an assault on the Momtaz. They race round a corner—but as they reach the door, their way is firmly but politely blocked by two burly Indian bouncers, totally unfazed by the troops.*

BOUNCER ONE
This is a private party sir. No lunches today.

*Inside the restaurant there is a Bangladeshi wedding in full musical swing. The noise is shaking the T in MOMTA_.*

COTTER
*(he pushes to the front, waves his badge)*
I'm a police officer. Let me in —

BOUNCER TWO *(helpfully)*
Ah, the Local Police. Yes, sir. The Meet Your Local Mafia Get-Together is this afternoon sir.
The time should be on your official invitation, sir.

COTTER
I demand to see the manager.

MANAGER *(Indian)*
*(promptly appears, very helpful, doesn't want trouble)*
You are a friend of the bride, sir? Or the groom?

COTTER
Neither. I want a girl called Chrissie.

MANAGER
Very Sorry, sir, no girls on Sunday, sir. —
Oh, you mean Missie Chrissie Lovelace.
Upstairs flat. Use side-entrance please.
No gentlemen callers after midnight, please sir.

COTTER
I am *not* a gentleman. I'm a policeman.
And I have a search warrant, damn you.
So open that door. *(pause)* And you said
"Lovelace"—what sort of a name is that?

MANAGER
Lovelace very distinguished noble name, sir.
Descended long line family sir—Lady Missie
Chrissie lots famous peoples sir friend royalty
she tell me Bonnie Charlie Harry whatnot—

*— mutters away as he slowly and elaborately unlocks the multiply padlocked side entrance and leads the increasingly impatient Cotter and several fully armed troops laboriously and slowly up the narrow rickety stairs to the upper flat.*

94. INT. CHRISSIE'S ROOM ABOVE MOMTAZ.

*It is empty. Except for a pair of panties on the bare floor near the wardrobe.*

MANAGER
Oh, she's left. And she'd paid the rent.
In advances. Very strange. Most unusual.

*Cotter gingerly picks up the panties and sniffs them.*

DEPUTY *(reprovingly)*
Dirty, Harry.

COTTER
Thought I recognised that perfume—
Got it! Winston. Brian Winston.

DEPUTY *(also sniffing at panties)*
Don't think so, sir. Passion Nights, I'd say.

COTTER *(rounds on manager)*
I don't suppose Missie Chrissie Lovelace left a
forwarding address, did she? No, don't bother.
I know precisely where she is. Follow me, men.

*Clouseau-fashion, they all try to pile down the narrow stairs again.*

## 95. EXT. LONDON STREETS.
*[Fast cutting sequence to music.]*

*The three scooters, red, white, and blue, are careering rapidly through
various well-known tourist spots, ostensibly en route from the Barbican
to the Russell Hotel, but in no actually possible but highly photogenic
order: Embankment, Marble Arch, Regents Zoo, The Mall, Trafalgar
Square, Lincoln's Inn Fields, etc. while (Italian Job tune) 'We are the
Film Conservation Society' plays loudly and cheerfully on the
soundtrack.*

## 96. EXT. OUTSIDE BRIAN'S HOUSE.

WRITTEN: *[Sting* title:]

4th Loo gRade

*Cotter and troops arrive in jeeps and police cars. Pile into the house.
Doors are easily busted open but then:
Numerous security devices are immediately activated. Home Alone in
hi-tech form. Have fun with imagining security devices. Slamming
doors. Metal shutters. Booby-traps. Electrified doorknobs. Digital dog
growls, lion roars, rugby chants. Sirens. Pepper spray. Etc. Finally :*

ROBOT VOICE *(Marvin. . .)*
Welcome to Winston Security. The sleeping gas
experience you are about to share is merely a
courtesy calling card while all doors are now locked
behind you and you wait for the police to arrive.
Happy dreams.

COTTER *(bellows at the robot voice:)*
We ARE the effing Police!

ROBOT VOICE
Well, why didn't you effing say so. Expect me to
know everything—Brain the size of a peanut—

*Cotter makes it to Chrissie's bedroom, as the gas disperses.*
*He finds Chrissie's suitcases. Takes out panties. Sniffs them.*

COTTER
That's them. I knew it.

DEPUTY *(kindly concern)*
Have you thought of getting treatment, sir.

COTTER
Winston. It has to be him. But where the hell is he?

DEPUTY
Hotel Russell, sir.

COTTER
How the hell do you know that?

DEPUTY *(produces a yellow stickie)*
Yellow stickie on his computer downstairs, sir.
"Meet Tom Bane. Hotel Russell. Sunday 12th
October. 11 a.m." Sir. Would you please stop
swearing, and sniffing panties, sir. There are
children in the audience. We hope.

COTTER.
I don't *give-a-dam. (Gone with Wind intonation)*
Meeting Tom Bane, eh. Let's hope we're not too
late. He's probably murdered him by now.

*Grabs an army comms device from one of the SAS soldierss,*
*tries to speak into it. Loud scrambling noises come back at him.*
*Gives up. Deputy hands him a very basic mobile phone. He calls:*

> COTTER
> Specialtry Branch? Yes, Cotter. Yes, reverse charges.
> Yes, the Aye Eye raid. What do you mean, nobody
> was there. So I forgot it was bloody Sunday. So, I
> have another raid for you. Yes, it's within budget.
> It's a hotel. I hope this is a secure line.

## 97. INT. HACKER'S DEN.

*Hacker is listening in, whistling cheerfully to himself.*

> HACKER
> Oh no it isn't. *(rings:)* Hello, Charlie. Me again.
> Next instalment. You owe me a bonus payment.

## 98. EXT. LONDON STREETS.

*The scooters are stopped at red traffic lights. A nearby TV shop is*
*showing the TV news on multiple screens. Alex sees shots of Frank*
*being escorted in his wheelchair. Gets off the scotter, takes helmet off.*
*Goes into the shop and listens:*

> TV: NEWS ANNOUNCER
> —the arrested man staged an instant protest
> demonstration when it became clear that the police
> station had no wheelchair access to the downstairs
> cells. *(shots of Frank at a police station, with a protest*
> *banner draped round his wheelchair : 'Access for All Souls to*
> *All Cells. NOW.')* Later, police made several raids in
> London and the Home Counties. They then issued
> several apologies. *(shots of the Momtaz Restaurant, then*
> *of the Aye Eye offices, with badly scorched but still intact*
> *doors)* Police are now reported to be looking for a
> man and two women in connection with their
> inquiries. *(mugshots of Chrissie & Debbie, then of Brian)*
> Police are already dubbing the wanted women

'The Most Wanted Women'. Mr Brian Winston is a
security consultant and a one-time government
employee. This is regarded as highly suspicious.
(the announcer listens to his ear-piece.) And we are
just receiving reports of another secret police raid,
about to take place, this time on a central London
Hotel, the Russell. (picture of the Russell Hotel).
We will of course bring you further news as soon as
we receive it from our sources.
Now, sport. And the England lacrosse team is in
deep trouble—

*Alex exits the shop, and leaves speedily on the scooter, while ringing
Brian's mobile number.*

> ALEX
> Er, Dad. Er, Have you seen the news? *(thinks)*
> Er, I hope you can still make it to lunch.
> We'll be at the, er, Regel, backwards. OK?

## 99. INT. RUSSELL HOTEL. LOBBY.

*Brian is still listening to Alex on his mobile phone as he makes his
way quickly down through the lobby, just as a heavily-equipped SAS
assault team try to get in through the front door. They are stopped by
the hotel staff. There is a packed Antiquarian Book Fair going on in
the main reception rooms. (This used to be a regular monthly event &
should be easily re-stageable, for a suitable donation to the ABA.)*

> MAJOR DOMO
> *(ever so slightly camp, but formidably in charge, he airily
> waves away all objections from the SAS commanding officer.)*
> And *where* do you think you're going with all those
> bags? Can't you read the notices. While the book
> fair is on, *all* bags have to be left at the cloakroom.
> *No* exceptions. Do you have your tickets. No?
> Right, back to the inquiry desk. There *is* a queue,
> you know. Cloakroom is on the left.

*Brian escapes through the bookfair as the SAS finally push past the
Major Domo and race up the stairs towards Bane's suite.
Great crashing sounds as they smash their way into everywhere.*

*Major Domo picks up the internal desk-phone, listens.*

> MAJOR DOMO
> I see. *(pause)* How much!? *(writes on a pad)*

*SAS troops come dashing down the stairs.*

*Major Domo stops the commanding officer as he tries to leave.
Presents him with a bill, on a silver platter.*

> MAJOR DOMO
> Your bill, sir. For the damage. VAT *is* included.
> But Serv-*ice est non compris.* We do accept all major
> credit cards. Except American Expresso.

*Officer angrily slams a credit card down on the silver tray and dashes
out. Major Domo pockets the credit card and throws the bill away.*

*Bane comes down the stairs with various flunkies.
He stops when he sees the book fair.*

> BANE
> Books. *Printed* books. Disgusting. Nobody told me
> there was a *book*fair on. God, I hate books.
> *(to flunkie)* Buy them. Buy them all. And pulp them.
> The fiction especially. Can't stand stories.

100. EXT. LONDON STREETS.

*Rapid sequence (long distance zoom lenses and overhead shots):
The three scooters, and Brian's car, are seen weaving in and out of
traffic towards Tate Modern. To Quadrophenia music.
In a very long shot, the three scooters go over the Blackfriars, Millenium
and Southwark Bridges—simultaneously.*

## 101. INT. POLICE SURVEILLANCE UNIT.

*Lots of monitors are showing CCTV coverage of all the famous streets of London. All are showing variations of Chrissie and Debbie in shot, at dozens of locations, simultaneously, including Mornington Crescent Tube Station.*

> OFFICER
> They're bloody well everywhere!
> We're being invaded! By lady clones!

## 102. INT. COTTER'S OFFICE.

> COTTER *(to weary Aide)*
> You heard what Hacker said. They were meeting
> at the Regal. Backwards. Uh, some code! Must be
> the name of a cinema. A cinema near you. Used to
> be dozens of them when I was a boy. Can't be *that*
> difficult to find one lousy cinema. Get onto it.

> AIDE
> But what does 'Backwards' mean, sir?

> COTTER
> How the, er, blazing saddles would I know?

## 103. FULL SCREEN. INT/EXT?

*Close up of Leger's Ballet Méchanique film: patterns, shapes, rhythms.*

*Show a few minutes and enjoy. Then pull back to show:*

## 104. INT. TATE MODERN. FILM ROOM.

*Alex, Debbie and Chrissie are sitting in the darkened room watching the Leger movie. Brian arrives to join them.*

> BRIAN
> Thought I'd find you here. Leger. Regal backwards,
> indeed. Ah, you must be Debbie.

*(he is very taken with her)* Er, can I take you to lunch?
I mean, I think it's time for lunch. For us all.
And some explanations?

105. INT. TOP FLOOR OF TATE RESTAURANT.
WONDERFUL VIEW OVER THAMES.

WRITTEN: [*Sting* title:]

> LUNCH AND SOME EXPLANATIONS.
> AT LAST. THE HUNCH.
> AND LAST ORDERS.

*It's the end of a very good meal, wine bottles, empty plates, etc.*
*Brian & Debbie are deep in animated discussion—about food.*
*Chrissie and Alex are amused but getting impatient.*

> ### BRIAN
> So how *do* you get a *boeuf bourguignon* really juicy?
> I never could. (*as if he'd ever tried!*)

> ### DEBBIE
> Matter of timing really. Make sure you brown the
> marinaded beef for no more than thirty seconds
> to begin with —

> ### CHRISSIE
> Could we forget about food for a few minutes,
> you two. There are more important things in life.
> Just at the moment.

> ### BRIAN
> Sorry, got rather carried away. OK.
> Let's begin with what we know. SoftCorp's launch
> of Patriarch seems to have created a new kind of
> warping virus, affecting a whole range of imaging
> systems: weather forecasting, military, radar,
> satellite navigation, even deep space telescopes.
> But how, and why? Patriarch is based on a set of
> neural nets originally developed by Aye Eye,

which SoftCorp stole from you. But how could a
neural net be infected by a virus?

ALEX
Am I going to understand this bit?

> BBC VOICE-OVER *almost sotto voce*:
Those viewers requiring immediate assistance
are encouraged to ask the people in the row
behind them. Loudly and inconsiderately.

DEBBIE
Well, Brian, our whole Artificial Intelligence system
was a network of neural nets, with three main
systems. One was called Paula, and that was the one
Bane stole from us. It's job was to compare,
collate and combine the outputs of the other two.
One, which I've still got, *(produces her laptop-umbrella,
coloured blue)* was Hugh, short for Greek Heurisko:
'I search'. Hugh's job was to find complex visual
matches among huge image-banks.

*She puts Hugh on the table and Chrissie puts Erika next to it.*

NB: *From now on, both laptops 'follow' the explanation, displaying
and exchanging appropriate illustrative images with each other,
while making cute little beeping and purring noises at each other.*

CHRISSIE
And the third system is my Erika, from 'eureka',
of course. She had to construct entirely new images
based on the matches produced by Hugh.

ALEX
Which is what *Rem-brand* does with portraits?

CHRISSIE
Precisely. Rem-Brand uses four of Hugh's search
criteria when he's looking for faces: eye-matches;
lip-matching, or synching; overall relative position

of eyes, nostrils, ears, and mouthline; and side
profiles. If all four match up, it's a pretty good bet
that the faces as a whole match.

DEBBIE
We developed other versions as well as Rem-Brand,
like 'Celeb-A-Clone': you'd feed into it all the
currently fashionable "Looks" and out would come
a marketing man's wet dream: the perfect 'celebrity'
you'd sort of half-recognise on an advertising
hoarding, but couldn't quite put a name to.

CHRISSIE
We even created some well-known politicians with
one version. We called it the 'Which Blair?' Project.

DEBBIE
Then we modified the Positioning net to look for
positions in star formations, or patterns of aircraft
flights, or landscape features like towns or roads on
satellite photos —

CHRISSIE
And the Profile sub-system developed into a
navigation device for matching outlines, like
coastlines, or the shapes of lakes and rivers —

DEBBIE
Put them all together and you had the basis of a
terrific set of applications. But there were problems.

CHRISSIE
Like, we tested the face recognition system on lots
of video footage of football hooligans, to see if it
could find the same people appearing in different
incidents.

BRIAN
And did it?

CHRISSIE

Sort of. It spotted the same police officers in plain clothes again and again. The undercover anti-hooligan squad. Which wasn't quite what we intended.

BRIAN

OK, that's an old issue with neural nets. How do you train them to produce the answers you actually want, not just results that fit. So what did you train Paula, Hugh, and Erika on?

ALEX *interrupts:*

I know! You used family photo albums, of you and Chrissie. Looking very different, at different ages, in lots of different contexts. Yes?

DEBBIE

Well spotted, kid! Chrissie used to love dressing up, so we had lots of photos of her in all sorts of costumes. Hugh had to find her in shots of kiddie's parties, or school outings, or fancy dress balls. Photos of me were easier to spot, but then Hugh had to decide between us, which was a bit trickier.

CHRISSIE

And Erika then had to display an accurate overall composite picture of Debbie or of me, but without any disguises.

ALEX

You mean strip away all the different make-up, costumes, clothes, er. . sorry.

BRIAN

OK, let me guess. In the final testing stages, instead of actual pictures of Chrissie or you, you just used short-hand binary code to trigger those matching searches.

DEBBIE
How on earth did you know that?

BRIAN
Because, Debbie, it was your birthday on Friday.
10th October. 10.10. One. zero. one zero. And the
first incident was triggered on 10th of the 10th at 10
hundred hours, the F16s. The second at 11.10, one
one one zero, the Stansted crisis. Binary code.
When Tom Bane stole your third machine,
it was that time-code plus your birthday-date
embedded in Paula's neural net, that triggered
SoftCorp's enormous systems to start looking
—but just for you and Chrissie. Paula was using the
whole Patriarch global search engine as a substitute
for Hugh and Erika. But Paula couldn't find you any
more.

CHRISSIE
You're right! SoftCorp didn't have our family album
in their databases, so Paula couldn't find us —

DEBBIE
— but did the best she could by *compositing* images
of us. In landscapes, the stars, weather patterns,
surveillance photos, ID databases—all the
applications SoftCorp had extended her to.

BRIAN
And she got even more confused when the date and
the time was yesterday: the 11th of the tenth, at
10.01, or 11.00, or 11.11, or 10.10. All of these sent
her into a flat spin, looking for and then making up
contorted versions of you both.

CHRISSIE
Yes. But now the big problem. How do we stop
her? Won't Paula just keep looking for us?

BRIAN

You'll have to somehow re-train the entire
Patriarch net-systems so they don't!

DEBBIE

I think you're right, Brian. But I'm stumped.
It's not like a piece of software. You can't just
re-write the program. You've got to somehow
re-jig the whole neural net. Re-train it. And then
reproduce that net in every one of SoftCorp's
servers. And that was the bit that always defeated
us. Before Bane stole the whole idea anyway.

BRIAN

So all the world's global imaging systems will just
continue to look for Chrissie and Debbie—
and not find you? Instead, they'll carry on making
up dream images of you. The whole world will just
be watching for you!

ALEX *(has been quiet, thinking)*

Hang on a minute. I think this might just work—
Look, Hugh and Erika are highly developed
artificial intelligences, yes. And up to now they've
been looking for their "Mummies", the people who
created them!—But what if they learned to look for
*themselves* instead. Their *own* identities. Can you give
Hugh the job of finding itself—himself. And Erika
the task of displaying that self, that image of
himself-herself?

BRIAN

But what's the image of an artificial intelligence?
Something that only exists as a configuration of a
neural net? That's a pretty abstract image!

ALEX

I know. I know. But listen: can you set up Hugh
and Erika to look for, and then create a face-match,

but one that *doesn't match* on *any* of the four features that make up a *human* face: the eyes, lips, positions, profiles.

DEBBIE
Sort of search on empty? *zero zero zero zero.*

CHRISSIE
But *where* do they search? What's the database?

ALEX
You'll see! Chrissie, do you still have those pictures from Kettles Yard on Erika? Let's start with those. Come on, and bring Hugh and Erika. They've got to carry on looking!

*Alex grabs Hugh and drags Chrissie, with Erika, away, leaving Debbie and Brian at the table. A Waiter comes over.*

WAITER
The enormous bill, sir? Just in case.
Word does get around.

BRIAN
Not yet. I think we'll have the suite trolley.
Do you do birthday cake?

WAITER
Well, we have an excellent layer cake, sir.

DEBBIE
That's very sweet of you, Brian.

BRIAN
I have a suspicion you may have to share it.


{Tea-break, anyone?}

106. INT. TATE MODERN.
VARIOUS GALLERY ROOMS.

*Very fast-forward: Alex and Chrissie are rapidly passing all the
abstract art in the Tate Modern galleries, happily taking digital snaps
with the built-in cameras on Erika and Hugh. Hugh and Erika are
cheerfully bleeping away, almost an excited tune. [Combines Russian
Ark and the race through the Louvre in Bande à part]*

107. INT. TATE RESTAURANT.

*Debbie and Brian are tucking into a huge layer cake.
Holding hands and gazing into each other's eyes, over the menu.
Alex and Chrissie return, with smug smiles. Interrupt.*

> DEBBIE
> Er, yes. OK, Alex, your Dad and I have been
> discussing, er, the technical logic of your hunch.
> We think it'll work. If you've really come up with
> a self-image for the whole system, we can feed that
> into all the SoftCorp databases, and then make the
> net search for *itself* as its default primary process.

> BRIAN
> So if it can find itself instead of trying to find
> Chrissie and Debbie, it can then happily go off
> and find any other things, as required.

> DEBBIE
> So do you two have something to show us?

> ALEX
> Aye aye, sir!

> CHRISSIE
> We think so.

*She sets Hugh and Erika down together on the table, linked together,
with Hugh's screen showing a subliminally rapid sequence of dozens of
abstract art images and Erika's showing the rapidly changing process
of the composite morphing of those image into one:*

*Suddenly Hugh's screen dwindles to a small dot.
And Erika triumphantly stabilises to display a dynamically changing
abstract image, a beautiful and gently modulating combination of:*

> Ben Nicolson
> Piet Mondriaan
> Cezanne
> Leger
> Braque
> Moholy Nagy
> Delaunay
> Klee
> Kandinsky
> Duchamps
> Kurt Schwitters
> Malevitch
> Pollock
> Johns
> Hodgkin
> Patrick Heron
> Miro
> Etc

*—all from Kettles Yard or Tate Modern. The ultimate screen-saver!*

CHRISSIE
Aaaah.

DEBBIE
How sweet.

BRIAN
That's AI for you: Abstract Imaging.

ALEX *(Frankenstein voice)*
It's alive! It's alive!

HUGH & ERIKA
*(singing in a beautiful madrigal harmony)*
Happy Birthday To I,
Happy Birthday To I.
Happy Birthday to I, I, *(etc)*

BRIAN
Birthday cake, anyone?

CHRISSIE
Right, and if we now change the binary trigger code,
the system will celebrate its very own birthday
*every* day of its little life!

HUGH & ERIKA
*(cheer wildly, with on-screen fireworks etc.)*

DEBBIE
It's time we talked to Mr Tom Bane. Hoots mon,
we have a solution. But you're gonna pay for it.

108. INT. CAR. COUNTRYSIDE

*Brief: on back seat, Chrissie and Alex. Chrissie has Erika on-line,*
*trying out various test searches. Each time the result is OK, and each*
*time the resulting image has a tiny logo in the corner of the screen.*
*Chrissie shows this to Alex by zooming in, and the logo is revealed as*
*a tiny clone of the AI self-portrait.*

*Front seat: Brian is driving. Debbie is on her mobile phone.*

DEBBIE
Got it? It's neutral territory. But on our terms.
OK. Eight o'clock. Be there.
*(to Brian)* Guess who's coming to dinner.

BRIAN
How come you have his personal phone number?

DEBBIE
Tell you some other time. *(smiles sweetly)*
When I know you a little better.

109. INT. MOMTAZ.

*Alex, Chrissie, Brian and Debbie at a long table.*
*Venkat is taking orders. Enter Frank in wheelchair, to cheers and*
*chants of: "Free Frankie Dickson" Hugs all round.*

FRANK
I think they were glad to see the back of me!
But thanks to whoever pulled the right strings.

ALEX
Dad, did you get Sir Gee Gee to help?

BRIAN
Well, he sorted out the charges against us four.
But after all that *other* stuff they found at Frank's,
he said Frank's case was way beyond him.
I thought it was Lord Anglia who rang the
Home Secretary or something.

DEBBIE
Hello, Frank. Heard a lot about you. I'm Debbie.
Chrissie's sister. *(a bit embarrassed)* Er, actually,
it was Chrissie and I. We rang Lady Anglia.
Who rang the Prime Minister. Who pulled a string
or two.

BRIAN
Lady Sybil? How is she involved?

CHRISSIE

She's our Mum.  Lord Anglia is her fourth husband.
She gets bored quickly. And the golf pro was a bit
of a mistake.

DEBBIE

The Home Secretary's her cousin anyway.
You see, she's the great-grand-daughter of Ida
Lovelace, who was Charles Babbage's first
computer programmer. For the Difference Engine.
And Ida Lovelace was also Lord Byron's daughter.
The poet. Connections. Make a difference. Still.

110. EXT. DARK NIGHT.

*A blinding white light in the black sky above.*
*The Light descends lower. Terrific noise. The blinding light is*
*— a helicopter. [Close Encounters]*

111. EXT. KING'S COLLEGE, GREAT COURT.

*Helicopter lands in the middle of the lawn. A Very Irate Porter*
*stalks across as Tom Bane gets out of the helicopter.*

PORTER

You can't park that thing there.
Only Fellows are allowed on the grass.

BANE

What's a Fellow? OK, OK, I'll pay the parking fine.
*(hands him a cheque)* Will that do?

PORTER *(looks at cheque)*

That will do *very* nicely, sir.

BANE

*(as they crouch under airflow of helicopter and head towards*
*the gate)* How do you get this grass so neat and tidy?

PORTER *(now amiable and obsequious)*
Well, sir, you turn over the soil. Level it—

BANE *(interrupts him)*
Yeah, I remember—four hundred years. Or so.
Now, where's this Mamma Caff place? I'm freezing!

PORTER
The Momtaz, sir? Just across the road, sir.
Next to the *Bouton Rouge*. You can't miss it, sir.

112. EXT. MOMTAZ.

*Sign is lit up. The 'T' has fallen off. Sign is now  MOM_A_ .*

113. INT. MOMTAZ.

*Alex, Chrissie, Debbie, Brian, Frank, Tom Bane.*
*Table is covered with legal papers as well as remnants of very large*
*Indian meal. Bane is concluding::*

BANE *(fast talking)*
OK, so we finally have a deal. I get the AI's
self-portrait image and licensed updates
to the Hugh and Erika nets from AI dot com.
Which Hugh and Erika will communicate in their
own sweet way to Paula, at a suitable meeting to be
arranged. In return, all SoftCorp image databases
from now on are to be copyright free.
And Patriarch is to be rebranded as *Leger*.
L-E-G-E-R  right? After some French painter guy.
That may be difficult to get through my PR people.
But OK. It's a deal. Done. Frank, if you ever want
a job at SoftCorp, just give me a bell. OK.

FRANK
I'll settle for your personal agent's personal phone
number instead. (pause) Lewis Carol's, sweet
Carolina's.  Your PA.

BANE

You spotted her, did you. OK? I'll ask her
to get in touch. Now I gotta get back to New York.
You can't escape from New York for long.

ALEX

Give my regards to MOMA.

BANE

Sure, kid. Look, I never travel with cash.
Can I leave the tab to you lot. Gotta dash.
'Copter's on a double yellow flower bed.  (*leaves.*)

*General relaxation.*

BRIAN

Coffees?  Or the bill??

CHRISSIE

I'll pick up the bill. Remember I get a discount.

ALEX

But Chrissie, you don't live here any more.

CHRISSIE

Yup, but I paid the rent in advance.

BRIAN *(cautiously, to Debbie)*

Er, you don't have to go back to London tonight,
do you? We do have another spare room.
If you want one.

ALEX *(to Chrissie)*

Chrissie, when's *your* birthday?

CHRISSIE

The 11th of November.

ALEX

I think I'll try and be out of the country.

BRIAN

Or off the planet.

114. INT. DINING ROOM. BRIAN'S HOUSE.

WRITTEN:

MONDAY MORNING,
SOMETIME MORE OR LESS AROUND
9 A.M. OR THEREABOUTS.

*Debbie is bringing through from the kitchen another round of superbly cooked breakfast. Deep satisfaction on Brian's face (not entirely due to breakfast).*

*Brian, Alex and Chrissie are reading various newspapers.*
*Various headlines and articles are visible:*

*Guardian:* Satanic Sitters Still On Run

*Sun:*  DIY Special Supplement!!
Introduction to Nueral Nexts:
Make Your Very Own Brain!!!

*FT:*  $10M donation to King's College, Cambridge.
Chill Bane Pays Windows Cleaning Bill.
Honorary Fellowship for Entrepreneur.

*Mirror:*  Crop Circle in Cambridge Quad!

BRIAN *(with covert glance at Debbie)*
Alex, school at nine. Time to get ready.
Let's get back to normal, please.

DEBBIE *(with covert glance at Brian)*
Haven't you got a ten o'clock lecture, Chrissie?

115. INT. ROOM. FIGURE AGAINST WINDOW.

> FIGURE
> *([to Sir Gee Gee on video-link)*
> Good effort, Gee-Gee. Nice cover story.
> So, we can all go back to work properly now.
> Just make sure we stay out of sight this time.
> Chrissie will have to work on her language chip.
> Oh, and ask Paula, Hugh and Erika to phone
> Home please. Big Daddy wants a word.

*An ungloved alien hand switches off the videophone.*

116. INT. HETI.

*Bored Assistant Two is glumly staring at screens.*
*Nothing doing.*

> ASSISTANT TWO
> Back to bloody normal, I suppose.
> The usual Great Big Nowt in the Sky.

*He turns his attention to the same Sudoku problem—and fails to*
*notice that several moving stars are tracing the shape of the River*
*Thames, as in the opening of East Enders.*
*A faint alien signature tune is just audible.*

117. INT. ALIEN CRAFT HIGH ABOVE EARTH.

*A Little Green Man alien commander is sitting at a control console.*
*Earth is visible through porthole.*
*The Commander opens an assigment folder.*
*(Same hand formation as Figure's.)*

*The Folder is one of a pile with discreet labels:*

> Vann,  Maurice
> Minor,  Minnie
> Hall,  Vaux

Rover, Land
Megan, Renauld
Baker, Stud A.
etc

*Inside the 'Ford, Anglia' folder is a photo of Lord Anglia.*

*Subtitled translation of alien gobbledygook speech:*

ALIEN COMANDER *(in alien)*
Oh no. Not him, again.

*Final shot of Planet Earth,*
*with a beaming Smiley face superimposed*
*(Melies, Journey to the Moon) and receding rapidly into space.*

FADE OUT

<u>THE END</u>

www.ingramcontent.com/pod-product-compliance
Lightning Source LLC
Chambersburg PA
CBHW060445040426
42331CB00044B/2611